Challenges of Discourse Processing

Challenges of Discourse Processing: The Case of Technical Documents

Edited by

Patrick Saint-Dizier

CAMBRIDGE
SCHOLARS
PUBLISHING

Challenges of Discourse Processing:
The Case of Technical Documents,
Edited by Patrick Saint-Dizier

This book first published 2014

Cambridge Scholars Publishing

12 Back Chapman Street, Newcastle upon Tyne, NE6 2XX, UK

British Library Cataloguing in Publication Data
A catalogue record for this book is available from the British Library

ISBN (10): 1-4438-5583-9, ISBN (13): 978-1-4438-5583-9

TABLE OF CONTENTS

LIST OF TABLES

PREFACE

The production of technical documents of various kinds is often considered in most industrial sectors as a costly and painful activity. Technical documents mainly include procedural texts (e.g. for maintenance, production launch), equipment and product manuals, various notices such as security notices, regulations (security, management), repositories of requirements and business rules (e.g. concerning the design properties of a product) and product or process specifications. Technical documents may be very large, with a complex conceptual structure; they often cover areas which are sensitive in terms of safety and security.

About two decades ago, technical documents have motivated a number of language processing research activities, with the development of authoring recommendations. In linguistics, the technical document genre was investigated in order to outline its language but also its cognitive and ergonomics properties. The new types of technical documents (e.g. requirements and business rules), the increasing constraints on technical documentation production and control (e.g. certifications, safety and security norms), and the emergence of more advanced needs (e.g. more accurate authoring recommendations, coherence controls between documents, traceability and update) require the development of a new generation of linguistic analysis and authoring tools. This is now made possible in particular thanks to the major developments of natural language processing methods, technologies, and resources over the last decade.

Discourse analysis still remains at the level of theoretical considerations with little application capabilities. The development of discourse annotation tools and methods may in the future allow the development of discourse parsers working with a good accuracy on a large diversity of types of documents. However, discourse analysis remains a very difficult and challenging area in natural language processing due to the complexity of discourse constructions whose analysis often involves language associated with domain knowledge and reasoning.

Technical documents are relatively constrained in terms of language diversity and complexity: the goal is to make sure that users can understand these documents without any ambiguity and therefore without any risk for their health or for the environment. Technical documents tend to minimize the distance between language and action: strategies to realize a goal are made as immediate and explicit as possible.

These considerations make it possible to develop an accurate discourse analysis of technical documents which can be used to improve their overall quality. From a more theoretical point of view, technical documents form a very interesting corpus of texts for discourse analysis. They allow the development of theoretical elements and tools for explanation and argumentation, two major aspects of discourse, which are crucial in technical documentation.

In this book, we show that linguistic analysis and natural language processing methods can efficiently and accurately be used to represent the discourse structure of technical documents and to improve their form and contents, independently of the industrial sector and activity. This book aims at presenting well-founded and concrete solutions, which can be deployed in industrial contexts.

The research from which this book emerged was funded by the French *Agence Nationale pour la Recherche* (ANR) from 2005 till 2013, via the TextCoop and then the Lelie projects. These two projects have motivated a large number of interactions with linguists, technical writers and researchers from the industry and academic circles involved in linguistics, computer science, document production and cognitive ergonomics. Collaborations in these various disciplines have allowed the development of useful principles and prototypes which are now been tested and customized in various industrial sectors. I thank our funding agency, the ANR, and my institution, the CNRS, for their continuous support. This book has also benefited from the work and the interactions with a number of researchers, users, technical staff and students. In particular, my special thanks to *Camille Albert, Farida Aouladomar, Florence Bannay, Flore Barcellini, Sarah Bourse, Estelle Delpech, Lionel Fontan, Marie Garnier, Corinne Grosse, Mathilde Janier, Juyeon Kang, Naima Khoujane and Marie-Christine Lagasquié.* I also want to thank the companies that helped us in our investigations, in particular: EDF, SNCF, EADS, Liebherr, Orange, and Thomson-Reuters.

CHAPTER ONE

AN INTRODUCTION TO THE STRUCTURE OF TECHNICAL DOCUMENTS

PATRICK SAINT-DIZIER

Introduction

Technical documents form a linguistic genre with very specific linguistic constraints in terms of lexical realizations and grammatical and style constructions. Typography and overall document organization are also specific to this genre. Technical documents cover a large variety of types of documents: procedures (also called instructional texts), which are probably the most frequently encountered in this genre, equipment and product manuals, various notices such as security notices, regulations (security, management), requirements (e.g. describing the design properties of a product) and product or process specifications. These documents are designed to be easy to read and as efficient and unambiguous as possible for their readers. For that purpose, these documents tend to follow relatively strict authoring principles concerning both their form and contents. However, depending in particular on the industrial domain, the required security level, and the target user, major differences in the writing and overall document organization quality can be observed.

An important feature is that technical documents tend to minimize the distance between language and action. Instructions to realize a goal are made as immediate and explicit as necessary, the objective being to reduce the inferences that the user will have to make before acting, and therefore potential hesitations, errors or misunderstandings. Technical documents are thus oriented towards action, they often combine instructions with icons, images, graphics, summaries, etc.

In this book, we mainly consider technical documents produced by the industry for their staff or for their industrial customers. Technical documents designed for the large public follow the same principles, but in a more shallow way. Procedures are documents designed to realize a certain task, possibly decomposed into subtasks. There are several types of tasks which can be described by procedures such as equipment installation or maintenance, production activities, and staff management. The size of a procedure ranges from one page for short notices to 200 pages. Procedures are written using various types of text editors, the most common one being Microsoft Word. Some large companies have their own authoring environment, in general based on XML. In that case, large hierarchies of XML documents may be produced and stored in text databases. The end-user gets in general a PDF document adapted to his task, or documents readable on tablets or on any equivalent electronic device, with the possibility to get additional information in an interactive way. Vocal applications also exist and are used e.g. when there is no possibility for operators to use a written support.

There is a large diversity of procedural texts, with different objectives and styles. In most cases, industrial procedures are rather uniformly composed of a hierarchy of titles that reflect a task-subtask hierarchy and instructions that describe how to realize each task or subtask. Titles and instructions form the backbone of procedures. A number of additional elements are often associated with instructions or subtasks in order to guide, help or warn the user in particular when there are difficulties or risks. We call these elements the *explanation structure of a procedure*. As will be seen in the next chapter, the explanation structure plays a major role in the correct realization of a task. The explanation structure includes, among others, definitions, illustrations, reformulations or elaborations, and also arguments such as warnings and advice. Explanation is aimed at providing users with information that may possibly partly contradict their beliefs or assumptions. Arguments do not provide any new information, they are designed to convince the user to realize the task as required.

Equipment and product manuals describe the structure or the composition and the properties of the equipment or product at stake, the precautions to take when using it, possibly how to store, install and maintain it. These documents have a rich structure, made of definitions and schemas, instructions, explanation and arguments.

Regulations and requirements form a specific subgenre in technical documents: they do not describe how to realize a task but the constraints that hold on certain types of tasks or products (e.g. safety regulations, management and financial regulations). Similarly, process or product specifications describes the properties or the expectations related to a product or a process which is being elaborated. These may be used as a contractual basis in the realization of the product at stake. Specifications often have the form of arguments.

Technical documents are seldom written from scratch: they are often the revision, the adaptation, or the compilation of previously written documents. Technical documents of a certain size are not produced by a single author: they result from the collaboration of several technical writers, technicians and validators. Their production may take several months, with several cycles of revisions, validation and updates e.g. coming from returns of experience from users. Their life cycle ranges in general between two and ten years. Text revision and update is a major and complex activity in industrial documentation, which requires very accurate authoring principles, text analysis and validation cycles to avoid any form of "textual chaos".

Elaborating a new technical document from previously existing ones is a major source of errors in spite of several proof-reading steps. These errors may result from incorrect updates, missing information, incorrect references, incorrect copy-paste operations, or from recent security norms which are not fully adapted to the situation described in the document. Therefore, technicians in operation or users must manage these deficiencies, e.g. finding errors and gaps, and elaborating by themselves alternative solutions. This is obviously a major source of stress, risk and accident. Controlling the quality of a document, in terms of form (from typography and general lay-out to style) and contents, is therefore essential to prevent risks, production errors and customer dissatisfaction. Quality analysis is also crucial to make sure regulations are enforced, or to get a certification or an adequate level of insurance.

In this book we show that linguistic analysis and natural language processing methods and tools can efficiently be used to analyse the form and contents of technical documents. Besides linguistic observations, this book aims at presenting concrete solutions for improving the form and contents of technical documents based on advanced, logic-based natural language processing techniques. This book focuses in particular on conceptual and discourse structure analysis within the context of technical documents, which is more restricted than in general language. Concrete solutions are addressed in depth in this book from a number of views that complement each other:

-First, some introductory considerations are presented on the typology of technical documents, on the way technical documents should be produced in interaction between authors and users, and on their global conceptual and discourse structure (Chapter 1, in the sections that follow).

- Then, the way a technical document is organized from a conceptual and a linguistic point of view is investigated: its discourse structure and in particular the title-instruction organization and also its explanation and argumentation structures since most technical documents offer a rich user support (Chapter 2).
-Next, the authoring recommendations that technical writers should follow in a number of companies are surveyed. Recommendations concern the uses of business terms, lexical choice, grammatical constructions and style (Chapter 3). These recommendations also reflect the principles developed for Controlled Languages.
-Then, Chapter 4 introduces the programming language Dislog that runs on a dedicated platform, <TextCoop>. Dislog is primarily designed for discourse processing. The discourse structures presented in Chapter 2 can be processed by this environment.
-The way to use this platform is explained in detail in Chapter 5, which is a kind of user manual.
-Chapter 6 is devoted to the linguistic structure of requirements and specification documents. These types of documents have a specific discourse structure which is outlined.
-Finally, in Chapter 7, the Lelie project is introduced. This project integrates most of the aspects presented above. The main aim of Lelie is risk prevention from an accurate analysis of the quality of written technical documents, in terms of form and contents. Risks include health as well as ecology or finance.

On the basis of a linguistic analysis that includes the lexical, grammatical, discourse and style levels and the use of natural language processing tools, this book aims at providing some essential technical answers to the following major challenges of technical documentation production:

- How to make sure that a technical document is written clearly and comprehensively enough to avoid any major risks (e.g. installation errors, task misconceptions, etc.)?
- How to make sure that technical documents can be accepted and used by technicians or end-users? This means that these documents are well understood, feasible, accepted, e.g. in terms of complexity and workload, and without any useless consideration.
- How to make sure that a technical document, and a procedure in particular, has a good internal coherence? This means that the instructions which are given allow an adequate realization of the goal(s) of the procedure.

-A last challenge is how to make sure that a procedure, via its instructions, follows the various public and business regulations it is concerned with?

Some Considerations on the Typology of Technical Documents

A technical document is a coherent set of statements whose goal is to reach a certain goal (for procedures and security requirements), to describe the properties and the way to use an equipment or a product, or to make more explicit the existing or expected properties of a system (e.g. using requirements) (Adam 1987). Technical texts may have different aims depending on their type, among which:

- ***Texts implementing regulations*** have a very efficient and injunctive form. A typical example are security notices (e.g. for fire prevention): these documents are very short and serve a very precise purpose. They describe in a very clear way the behaviour of the reader when the situation at stake occurs. The style is simple, direct and very injunctive.
- ***Texts having a "programmatic" nature:*** their goal is mainly to offer a structured knowledge on a given topic: use of an equipment, development of a know-how, or description of the elements to prepare, use or elaborate in a given situation. The form of these texts can be made quite flexible and attractive to the reader. Various forms of illustrations are frequently used.
- ***Procedural texts***: describe how to realize a precise action by means of temporally ordered instructions. Large companies have in general their own authoring recommendations that technical writers must follow.
- ***Texts describing the design or the functional properties*** of systems or equipment (design requirements) (Hull et al. 2011). Their style follows very precise guidelines, sentences are short and as unambiguous as possible since it is crucial to avoid any type of misunderstandings that would lead to incorrect products or product uses.
- ***Advice texts:*** are less strictly written and organized (no temporal structure a priori). These include texts devoted e.g. to staff management, meeting organization, social behaviour in companies or with customers.

Elements of an Analysis of the Gaps between Technical Writers and Operators

When investigating the form of technical documents, a major point is to observe how technical writers proceed when they elaborate a document. This means investigating technical document validation steps, how their life cycles are implemented, and possibly how returns of experience are taken into account. In document production, the emphasis is more frequently put on the producer than on the consumer, while the latter should in fact be the most important parameter of the process. We present here a short analysis of the gaps that often exist between technical writers and technicians in operation. These latter often have to find solutions to errors or gaps they find in technical documents. This is obviously a stressful situation that may lead to accidents. In the maintenance domain, about 78% of the technicians recognize that they found errors in procedures and that they had to elaborate alternative solutions without any external support. This clearly shows the difficulty of the task since even experienced technical writers encounter difficulties to produce stable and comprehensive documents. It is interesting to note that a number of technical writers have a strong experience as operators.

A number of investigations in cognitive ergonomics, based on precise protocols, have analysed problems of adequacy and efficiency of written procedural texts. The analysis was realized on the global structure of a procedure as well as on the structure of every instruction (e.g. (Schriver 1989)). The main reasons of a lack of adequacy and efficiency can be summarized as follows:

- A partial incompatibility between the document structure and the mental model of the operator who has to convert written instructions into actions. For example, an instruction may need to be decomposed into several concrete actions or, vive-versa, a set of instructions needs to be grouped to form a single action. The temporal organization of instructions may also be somewhat adapted to a given situation by the operator.
- An insufficient consideration for human factors (such as complexity of an action, communication in a noisy environment, isolated worker situation) that generates stress and psychological and social problems. Similarly, an inadequate or insufficient analysis of the various returns of experience produced by operators generates frustration.

- The difficulty and the stress associated with unexpected situations that operators often have to manage alone and in emergency situations.

These elements are essential and must accurately be taken into account when producing technical documents. However, besides authoring guidelines that need to be improved, user reactions must be taken into account and anticipated.

Towards the Elaboration of Quality Criteria for Technical Documents

In Chapter 3 of this book, we present criteria to improve the quality and ease of use of technical documents. These criteria are elaborated from the observation of technical writers at work, e.g. how they interact between each other and with technicians, and then how technicians read and analyse the technical documents that they use. These observations are paired with recommendations produced within the framework of ***Controlled languages*** (e.g. (Weiss 1991), (Alred 2012), (O'Brien 2003), (Wyner et al. 2002), see also internet links in the bibliography section). Note that controlled language guidelines operate only at the "surface" level of documents, not at the contents level.

Another difficulty is that, quite often, large documents are produced by teams of technical writers, who spend a lot of time revising text portions written by their colleagues. Revising such documents raises problems of competence and responsibility. Finally, when writing guidelines are very strict, it turns out that they are not strictly followed in a number of cases. On the other hand, when they are too shallow, they are not taken into account seriously. Therefore, there if a tradeoff to find between these two extremes when developing guidelines.

Technical documentation production can be realized according to two very different perspectives: (1) either the technical writer is strongly guided and has little choice in the constructions and terms he can use, this is the language technology proposed in the *boilerplates* perspective or (2) he can write documents with a certain freedom, following authoring principles, and with an *a posteriori* control on what he has written. The first perspective is relevant e.g. for requirements (Chapter 6). Boilerplates are indeed used for producing very simple documents such as security notices or for producing software requirements, which must follow extremely simple structures. The boilerplate technology is not adapted to the production of large and often complex procedures, where a certain flexibility in language must remain the rule. In that case *a posteriori* controls are much more adapted and better accepted by authors.

Let us review here a few general principles concerning document production quality criteria that we have elaborated from the literature and our observations, these are further developed and illustrated in Chapter 3. The motivation for high quality documents is often to limit the cognitive load imposed to the operator when he reads the document. The main criteria are:

-***Statements simplicity:*** clear, precise and non-ambiguous terms in the domain considered must be used with a syntax as elementary as possible. In an instruction, for example, the verb *count* will be preferred to a verb such as *observe* since this latter verb does not correspond a priori to a precise action. Lists of preferred terms are often given in company's guidelines. Statements are preferably in the active voice, with the verb complements in their canonical order (i.e. as expected by the verb "base" form).

- ***Statements conciseness***: useless words or constructions (modals, auxiliaries) must be avoided, long expressions must be replaced by shorter ones when the meaning is not affected.

- ***Document cohesion***: the design of the document, as well as its style and grammatical constructions must be used in a homogeneous way. Links between paragraphs must be clear and stable. Tables, legends and graphics must be organized in similar ways. Abbreviations, units and other such elements must always be used in the same way, with no variants.

- ***Clarity of the main elements***: the main elements, instructions, goals, warnings, etc. should be the most visible, possibly with an adequate typography. Words which are too general have in general a relatively empty or vague meaning (*impact, interface*). These words must be avoided. Similarly, pronouns with unclear references or fuzzy terms must not be used.

- ***Accessibility and readability*** of the document: the text must be easy to read and to understand by the target user, using words and constructions he masters.

These principles apply to any type of technical document. Product specifications and safety and design requirements may be associated with additional recommendations which are proper to the activity they are related to.

Some Considerations on the Conceptual and Discourse Structures of Technical Documents

A few Conceptual Principles

Technical documents are specific forms of documents, satisfying constraints of economy of means, expressivity, precision and relevance. They are in general based on a specific logic and type of organization, made up of presuppositions, implicit goals, causes and consequences, inductions, warnings, anaphoric networks, etc. They also include more psychological elements (e.g. *to stimulate a user*). The goal is to optimize the logical sequencing of instructions and make the user feel safe and confident with respect to the goal(s) he has to achieve (e.g. *clean an oil filter, learn how to organize a customer meeting*).

Procedural texts, from this point of view, can be analyzed not only as sequences of mere instructions, but as efficient, one-way (i.e. no contradiction, no negotiation) argumentative discourses, designed to explain to a user how to realize a task, providing motivations and helping him to make the best decisions at each step of his work. This type of discourse contains a number of facets, which are often associated in a certain way with explanation. Procedural discourse is indeed informative, explicative, descriptive, injunctive and sometimes narrative and figurative. These features are used with large variations depending on the author, the activity and the target reader. From that point of view, given a certain goal, it is of much interest to compare or contrast the means used by different authors, possibly for different audiences.

Writing a procedure and producing explanations is a rather synthetic activity whose goal is to use the elements introduced by knowledge elicitation mechanisms to help the user to acquire additional knowledge or revise his skills, beliefs and knowledge when these are not fully correct or up to date. Explanation may also induce generalizations, subsumptions, deductions, and the discovery of relations between objects or activities and the goals to reach. Argumentation does not a priori entail the acquisition of new information: it is designed to convince the reader that the procedure as it is written is among the best ways to realize it in a safe, efficient and economical way.

The authors of technical documents must consider three dimensions (Donin et al., 1992), (Van der Linden 1993) when producing such a document:

(1) ***cognitive***: it is essential to make sure that notions referred to are well-mastered and understood by the target users,

(2) ***epistemic***: it is crucial to take into account, possibly to deny them, the beliefs of those users, and
(3) ***linguistic***: it is necessary to use an appropriate language. This means, as already advocated, to adjust to the target user the accuracy of words, the technical level, the complexity of sentences and paragraphs, and the visual and typographic structure of the text.

The authors of technical documents start from a number of assumptions or presuppositions about potential users, about their knowledge, abilities and skills, but also about their beliefs, preferences, opinions, ability to generalize and adapt a situation, perception of generic situations, and ability to follow discursive processes. For example, users must often adapt instructions to their own situation, which is not exactly the situation described in the procedure. The producers of procedural texts have, from this basis, to re-enforce or weaken presuppositions, to specify some extra knowledge and know-how, and possibly to outline incorrect beliefs and opinions. They have to convince the reader that his text will certainly lead to a successful realization of the task at stake, modulo the restrictions they state (Aouladomar 2005).

Technical documents are in general highly structured and modular. They exhibit a particularly rich micro-rhetorical structure integrated into the syntactic-semantic structures of instructions. Procedural texts are a particularly difficult exercise to realize. For example they must make linear, because of language constraints, actions which may have a more complex temporal or causal structure. Connectors and referents contribute to implement this linearity, making the task simpler. Texts are also expected to be locally and globally coherent, with no contradictions, and no space for hesitation or negotiation.

Another important feature, which is rather implicit, is the way instructions or groups of instructions are organized and follow each other, and how the logic (objective aspect) and the connotations (subjective aspects) that underlie this organization (sequential, parallel, concurrent, conditional, multi-user, etc.) cooperate to produce optimal documents. The general organization of a document, its lay-out and its typography contribute to optimize its use. Going one step further, the relation between text and pictures, diagrams or images, which is not addressed in this book, is an important issue in technical documents. Pictures and diagrams complement or illustrate the text, they facilitate understanding via a visual support but may also raise ambiguities.

Finally, there is most of the time no syntactic sign characterizing the author or the user: there is no use of personal pronoun like "You" or "We". However, the author is implicit in languages such as French or Spanish by the use of imperative or infinitive verbal forms. The most common form used by authors to express instructions is the injunctive discourse. It characterizes several modalities of discourse: orders, preventions, warnings, avoidances, advice. These all have a strong volitional and deontic dimension. Injunctive discourse shows how the author of an instructional text imposes his point of view to the user: instructional texts are a prototypical example of a logic of action. Injunction is particularly frequent in security notices or in any difficult task where security is important. The strength of an injunctive statement is measured via the illocutionary force of the statement, often realized by verbs combined with adverbs.

A Global Analysis of the Structure of Procedures

The structure of most technical documents is highly hierarchical and very modular. These documents often follow authoring and organization principles proper to a company or to an organization that specify how to organize the different levels of the document.

The higher level of technical documents often starts by a few introductory words defining the task described in the document. These words are associated with general considerations such as purpose or motivations, scope, limitations and context. This higher level also contains a date of issue, a table of contents, a list of contributors and indications about revisions carried out, its maturity status and its distribution or confidentiality level. It can then be followed by definitions, examples, scenarios or schemas. A technical document often ends by annexes and a set of references, e.g. to previous documents or to external documents where more information can be found about a precise topic or equipment.

Lower levels include a hierarchy of sections that address the different facets of the goals the document proposes to achieve. Each section may include for its own purpose general elements similar to those given above followed by the relevant instructions. Instructions can just be listed in an appropriate temporal order or be preceded by comments. Each instruction or group of instructions can be associated with e.g. conditions or warnings, goal expressions and forms of explanation such as justifications, reformulations or illustrations.

The temporal aspects in a procedure are important. In general, to facilitate their execution, instructions describe actions that strictly follow each other, in a very clear linear order. However, there are cases that involve partial or total instruction overlap. Some actions are also triggered by others or must show a certain degree of synchronization; they must therefore be explicitly related by an appropriate connector (e.g. *heat the probe till it reaches 80 degrees and then stop the electricity*). Except for these latter cases where it is clearly stated, temporal connectors are often not explicit. They are often realized by punctuation marks, the ambiguous "*and*" or the simple succession of instructions.

Depending on the complexity of the task to realize, the risks and the technical level of the operator, instructions may be associated with more or less textual information. Instructions may also be marked as optional or they may need to be repeated till a certain condition is reached.

Each instruction in a procedure may be realized as a sentence or, equivalently, as an element of an enumeration. Quite frequently, instructions are grouped by small units which share a number of parameters (objects, conditions, goals, etc.). These instructions are realized in a single sentence with the use of referents or ellipsis (e.g. *before you start, you must open the box, clean its interior and plug in the white cable).* We call this small group of instructions an instructional compound, which is often considered as a single operational unit.

Considering the structure of instructions, two main works introduce the major foundational aspects of instruction contents. These will be used as the starting point of the development of the discursive structure of procedural texts that we have elaborated and which is developed in Chapter 2. First, (Bieger et al., 1984-85), based on a cognitive approach, propose a taxonomy of the contents of instructions organized in nine points:

-inventory (objects and concepts used),
-description or definition (of objects and concepts),
-operational (information that suggest the agent how to realize an action) such as manners or means to use,
-spatial (spatial data about the actions, how they follow each other or how they are combined in a spatial environment),
-contextual aspects,
-covariance (of actions, which must evolve in conjunction),
-temporal aspects,
-qualificative (limits of an information), and
-emphatic (redirects attention to another action).

The second investigation we consider was realized within the framework of Computational Linguistics, it is due to (Kosseim, 2000). She isolated from corpus analysis nine main structures or operations, called *semantic elements*. These partly overlap or complement the previous ones, with a more operational view of procedures:

-sequential operations: a necessary structured group of actions that the agent must realize,
-object attribute: description meant to help understand the action to realize, with what means or objects,
-material conditions: concrete environment in which an action must be carried out,
-effects: consequences of the realization of a group of operations on the world (or environment of the user),
-influences: explain why and how an operation must be realized and its consequences on others,
-co-temporal operations: express operation synchronization, overlap, or any other temporal organization,
-options: optional operations, designed to improve the quality of the results, these are called advice in our terminology. Optionality may receive several degrees.
-preventions: describe actions to avoid, these are called warnings in our terminology,
-possible operations: possible operations to do in the future, such as evaluations or controls.

As the reader may note it, the internal structure of instructions may be quite complex. An instruction is not just an action composed of a main verb, an object and an instrument, but it is often the conjunction of many conceptual elements which are necessary for a correct execution of the action(s). A number of these elements are formalized in the next chapter, Chapter 2, where their grammatical and discourse structures are investigated. Principles and recommendations on how to write instructions are given in Chapter 3.

The goal of this introductory chapter was to give an overview of technical documentation production and technical document overall structure. The chapters that follow investigate some of the problems advocated here; they propose solutions based on linguistic analysis and natural language processing tools. These chapters can be read independently.

CHAPTER TWO

THE LANGUAGE OF TECHNICAL DOCUMENTS: A LINGUISTIC DESCRIPTION OF ARGUMENTATION AND EXPLANATION

PATRICK SAINT-DIZIER

Introduction and Context

In this chapter we investigate the linguistic structure of technical documents. We focus in particular on the structure of procedural texts since it is the most central and crucial document in the industry, but the elements presented here are also applicable to the other types of technical documents, such as requirements, which are developed in Chapter 6. As indicated in Chapter 1, procedural texts cover a large diversity of categories of texts, with various styles, e.g. maintenance and installation of equipment, security guides, medical notices, social behavior recommendations, management guides and legal documents. Several features of the present chapter have been initially developed in (Bourse and Saint-Dizier 2012).

Procedural texts consist of a sequence of instructions, designed with some accuracy in order to reach a goal (e.g. *assemble a computer*). Procedural texts often include sub-goals (e.g. *dealing with the different subparts of a computer*). Goals and sub-goals are most of the time linguistically realized by means of a hierarchy of titles and subtitles. The objective is that the user must carefully follow step by step the goal / sub-goals structure and the instructions in order to correctly realize the task at stake. The general conceptual structure of technical documents is presented in Chapter 1.

Analyzing the structure of procedural texts means identifying titles (which convey the main goals of the procedure), sequences of instructions serving these goals, and a number of additional structures such as prerequisites, warnings, advice, illustrations, evaluations, reformulations, etc. (Van der Linden 1993), (Takechi et ali. 2003), (Adam, 2001). Procedural texts follow a number of structural criteria, whose realization may depend on the author's writing abilities, on the target user, and on traditions or recommendations associated with a given domain. Procedural texts, as introduced in Chapter 1, can be regulatory, procedural, programmatory, prescriptive or injunctive.

Procedural texts are complex structures, they often exhibit quite a complex structure with both rational (the instructions) and "irrational" aspects, mainly composed of advice, warnings, contextual restrictions, conditions, expression of preferences, evaluations, reformulations, user stimulations, etc. These latter form what we call the ***argumentative and explanation structures***; they motivate and justify the goal-instructions structure, viewed as the backbone of procedural texts.

Argumentation includes in particular advice and warnings. Argumentation is very useful, sometimes as important as instructions. Arguments are designed to motivate the user to realize the task as explained, otherwise he may undergo some difficulties or risks. Explanation provides a strong and essential internal coherence to procedural texts: while arguments are designed to convince a user to realize a task are required, explanation provides additional knowledge to the user, possibly in contradiction with his beliefs. Argumentation and explanation complement each other.

From a theoretical point of view, the structure of technical texts may be represented by means of rhetorical relations (Rhetorical structure theory, RST (Mann and Thomson 1988 and 1992)). The relations presented in this chapter are close to RST relations, but they are at the same time simpler and more specific to the technical document genre. In this book, we briefly address RST features in general since they are well developed in the literature (e.g. (Taboada et al. 2006), (Taboada, 2006)).

An important aspect of this chapter is the accurate identification of the explanation structures and the communication goals they serve in procedural texts in order to better understand explanation strategies deployed by technical writers in precise, concrete and operational situations, so that they can be improved and reproduced in other contexts.

The analysis reported in this chapter was carried out on a development corpus of about 200 French and English texts from various industrial sectors, in particular: chemistry, energy, transportation, health, food processing, etc.

This chapter gives some foundations for argumentation and explanation in terms of structure and functions within the framework of technical documents. We first introduce the notion of explanation in general, as it has been addressed in the literature and then address the current discourse analysis challenges since argumentation and explanation are very much related to discourse. Argumentation being a complex area, we present in this book its uses in technical texts. In a second stage, we introduce the functions that explanation plays in technical documents, which is much more restricted and controlled than in ordinary circumstances. For that purpose, we introduce the notion of elementary explanation functions, as observed from corpus analysis and common practices given in authoring recommendation manuals. Explanation schemes, which are the language realizations of explanation functions are then introduced. This chapter ends by a relatively detailed analysis of a number of discourse structures which are the most prominent in argumentation and in explanation schemes. These structures are given in a standard grammatical form. Chapter 4 and 5 show how these structures can be used in an automatic analysis of discourse structures. In Chapter 6, these structures will be considered again to account for the structure of requirements, which is a specific activity in technical document production.

Argumentation in Action

Argumentation is found in the description of goals, alternative choice statements, warnings, and within instructions. The four major forms of arguments frequently found in procedures (Aouladomar 2005) are described below. Verb classes referred to are in general those specified in WordNet (Fellbaum 1998). At this stage a few linguistic marks and syntactic schemas are given. These are investigated in more depth at the end of this chapter.

Arguments related to goals are the most frequent ones. They usually motivate a goal implemented as a subtask, a set of instructions or more locally an instruction. They must not be confused with purpose clauses: their role is to justify the action, outlining the importance of that goal, the potential risks and difficulties. Their general syntax is the following:

(1) purpose connectors + infinitive verbs,

(2) causal connectors + deverbal or

(3) titles, with a causal or a purpose connector: *to, for in order to*,

e.g. do X *to remove safely the bearings*, make Y *for a correct cleaning of the universal joint shafts*.

Prevention arguments: are based on a "positive" or a "negative" formulation. Their role is basically to explain and to justify an instruction or a group of instructions. Negative formulations are easy to identify, they are realized by one of the following syntactic schemas:

(1) negative causal connector + infinitive risk verb,
(2) causal connectors + modal + VP(infinitive verb),
(3) negative causal mark + risk verb,
(4) positive causal connector + VP(negative form),
(5) positive causal connector + prevention verb.

The grammatical and lexical elements in these constructions are in particular:

– negative connectors*: otherwise, under the risk of*, (e.g. *otherwise you may damage the connectors*).
– risk verb class*: risk, damage*, etc. (e.g. *in order not to risk the user's life*).
– prevention verbs: *avoid, prevent*, etc. (e.g. *in order to prevent the card from skipping off its rack*).
– positive causal mark and negative verb form: *in order not to*, (e.g. *in order not to make it too bright, in order not to spoil the fruit*).
– modal SV: *may, could*, (e.g. *because it may be prematurely worn due to the failure of another component*).

Positive formulation marks are the same as for the arguments related to goals described above, with the following syntactic schemas:

(1) purpose mark + infinitive verb,
(2) causal subordination mark + subordinate proposition,
(3) causal mark + proposition,

with:

– purpose marks: *so as to, for*,
– causal marks: *because, this is why*, etc.
– causal subordination marks: *so that, for.*
– the verbs encountered are usually of "conservative" type *: preserve, maintain,* etc. (e.g. *so that the axis is maintained vertical*)

Performing arguments: are less imperative than the previous ones, they express advice or evaluations. Their corresponding syntactic schemas are:

(1) causal connector + performing NP,
(2) causal connector + performing verb,
(3) causal connector + modal-performing verb,
(4) performing proposition.

Resources or structures are, for example:

– performing verbs: *allow, improve*,
– performing NP: (e.g. *for a better performance, for more competitive fares)*

– performing proposition: (e.g. *have small bills, it's easier to tip and to pay your fare that way*).

Threatening arguments: have a strong impact on the user's attention when he realizes the instruction, the risks are made very clear via very injunctive schemas. These arguments follow one of the following syntactic schemas:

(1) otherwise connectors + consequence proposition,

(2) otherwise negative expression + consequence proposition,

with, e.g.:

– otherwise connectors: *otherwise*,

– otherwise negative expression: if … do not … (e.g. *if you do not pay your registration fees within the next two days, we will cancel your application*)

Besides these four main types of arguments, some forms of stimulation-evaluation (*what you only have to do now...*) and evaluation can be found.

Explanation in Action

Explanation and its relations to language, cognition and linguistics is a relatively new and vast area of investigation. Explanation analysis involves the taking into account of a large number of aspects, e.g. typography, syntax, semantics, pragmatics, domain and contextual knowledge, and user profile.

At the moment, explanation is essentially developed in sectors where didactics is involved, e.g. writing recommendations for producing essays or, in interactive environments, in systems such as helpdesks. In artificial intelligence, explanation is often associated with the notion of argumentation (Reed 1998) and (Walton et al. 2008), but argumentation is just one facet of explanation. Let us also note investigations on causality, and an emerging field around negotiation and explanation in multi-agent systems associated with an abstract notion of belief (Amgoud et al. 2001). Two decades ago, simple forms of explanation were used to produce natural language outputs for experts systems, often from predefined templates. The goal was to justify why a certain proof was produced and why a certain solution was proposed as a result of a query. In the same range of ideas, natural language generation planning made some use of explanation structures, e.g. (McKeown 1985).

Interesting principles have emerged from these works which have motivated the emergence of interdisciplinary research. For example, in ergonomics and cognitive science, the ability for humans to integrate explanation about a task described in a document or on an electronic device (possibly via a guidance system) when they perform that task is investigated and measured in relation with the document properties (Lemarié et al. 2008), (Bieger and Glock 1984). In linguistics, a lot of efforts have been devoted to the definition and the recognition of discourse frames (Webber et al. 1990, 2004) (Miltasaki et al. 2004) (Saito et al. 2006) and the linguistic characterization of rhetorical relations (Mann and Thompson 1988; 1992), (Longacre 1982), which are, for some of them, central to explanation (Rösner and Stede 1992), (Van der Linden 1993). However, we now observe a proliferation of rhetorical relations with various subtleties, which, for some of them, turn out to be quite difficult to recognize solely on the basis of language marks since they involve quite a lot of pragmatic considerations and domain knowledge. Finally, explanation is a field which is investigated in pragmatics, e.g.: cooperativity principles (Grice 1978), dialogue organization principles and speech acts, e.g. (Searle et al. 1985), explanation and justification theory (Pollock 1974) and in philosophy, e.g.: rationality and explanation, phenomenology of explanation, causality (Keil and Wilson 2000), (Wright 2004) and, with a perspective on action, (Davidson 1980).

Explanation is in general structured with the aim of reaching a goal. This goal may be practical (e.g. how to reach a certain location) or more interpersonal or epistemic (e.g. convince someone to do something in a certain way, negotiate with someone while providing explanation about one's point of view). Explanation is in fact often associated with a kind of instructional style, explicit or implicit, which ranges from injunctive to advice-like forms. Procedures of various kinds (social recommendations, do-it-yourself (DIY), maintenance procedures, health care advice, didactic texts) form an excellent source of corpus to observe how explanation are constructed, linguistically realized and what aims they target.

Procedures are of much interest to build a corpus for explanation analysis since the language which is used is often simple and direct. Indeed, procedures are essentially oriented towards action: there must be little space for inferences. This kind of corpus is particularly well-adapted for our investigation and for the development of stable generalizations: it covers quite a large proportion of situations which are reproducible, e.g. in authoring tools, helpdesks or in natural language generation systems.

Explanation occurs also in a large variety of goal-driven but non-procedural contexts, for example, as a means to justify a decision in legal reasoning, in political discourse and debates, as a way to explain the reasons of an accident in insurance accident reports or as a form of synthesis of an evaluation in opinion expression. Explanation may also be associated with various pragmatic effects (irony, emphasis, dramatization, etc.) for example in political discourse. In each of these cases, explanation does keep a goal-oriented structure as developed in (Carberry 1990), (Takechi et al. 2003).

Explanation analysis and production is essential in opinion analysis to make more explicit how a certain opinion is supported (Garcia-Villalba et al. 2012), it is also essential in question answering systems when the response which is produced may not be the direct response: the user must then understand via appropriate explanation why the response provided is appropriate (Benamara et al. 2004). Finally, it is central in a number of types of dialogues, clarification situations, persuasion strategies, etc.

Our main goal is to identify a number of prototypical, widely used, explanation schemes, their linguistic basis (e.g. prototypical language marks or constructs), and to categorize their underlying communicative goals. We aim at identifying the language and pragmatic means, given a certain aim, which are used to help, support, motivate or convince a reader. This is obviously a very large task with a number of semantic as well as pragmatic issues which are very difficult to capture and to model.

In this chapter, we introduce the notion of ***explanation function*** that specifies a number of simple communicative goals which may be supported by explanation. Explanation functions are abstract constructs which are realized in language via what we call ***explanation schemes***. An important feature is that these schemes are trans-categorial: they include syntactic and lexical semantics factors, as well as typographic and pragmatic factors. Images, diagrams, and other multimedia devices are not considered here.

Discourse Analysis Challenges

Discourse structure analysis is a very challenging task because of the large diversity of discourse structures, the various forms they take in language and the impact of knowledge and pragmatics in their identification. Recognizing discourse structures cannot in general only be based on purely lexical or morphosyntactic considerations: subtle kinds of knowledge associated with reasoning schemas are often necessary. These latter capture the various facets of the influence of pragmatic factors in our understanding of texts (Kintsch 1988), (Di Eugenio et al. 1996).

The importance of structural and pragmatic factors required for discourse analysis does depend on the type of relation investigated, on the textual genre and on the author and targeted audience. In our context, technical texts are obviously much easier to process than literary or free-style texts. In most situations linguistic cues are explicit, in particular at the lexical, morphological, typographic or syntactic levels. This is developed in the next sections.

In contemporary linguistics, rhetorical structure theory (RST) (Mann et al. 1988, 1992) is a major attempt to organize investigations in discourse analysis, with the definition of 22 basic structures. Since then, almost 150 relations have been introduced which are more or less clearly defined. Background information about RST, annotation tools and corpora are accessible at *http://www.sfu.ca/rst/.* A recent overview is developed in (Taboada et al 2006) and a global architecture for discourse processing and the structure of marks are given in (Stede 2012).

Very briefly, RST poses that coherent texts consist of minimal units, which are all linked to each other, recursively, through rhetorical relations. No unit is left pending: all units must be connected to some others. Some text spans appear to be more central to the text purpose, these are called ***nuclei*** (or kernels), whereas others are somewhat more secondary and are semantically linked to the more central ones, they are called ***satellites***. Satellites must be associated with at least one nucleus.

Relations between nuclei and satellites are one-to-one or one-to-many. For example, an argument conclusion may have several supports, possibly with different orientations. Conversely, a given support can be associated with several distinct conclusions.

For example, in the sentence:

To prepare such a tart, you need red fruits, for example, strawberries or raspberries...

the discourse relation "illustration" is composed of a nucleus:

red fruits

and a satellite, which is the list of such fruits:

strawberries, raspberries.

Note that these two structures are not necessarily adjacent. Similarly:

prepare a tart and *red fruits*

are in a "prerequisite" or "specialization" relation, where the latter is the satellite, the nucleus being expressed as a goal.

The literature on discourse analysis is particularly abundant from a linguistic point of view. Several approaches, based on corpus analysis with a strong linguistic basis are of much interest for our purpose.

Discourse relations are investigated together with their linguistic marks in works such as (Delin 1994), (Marcu 1997, 2002), (Kosseim et al. 2000) with their usage in language generation in (Rosner et al. 1992), and in (Saito et al. 2006) with an extensive study on how marks can be acquired. A deeper approach is concerned with the cognitive meaning associated with these relations, how they can be interpreted in discourse and how they can trigger inferential patterns, e.g. (Wright 2004), (Moeschler 2007) and (Fiedler 2001) just to cite a few works.

Within Computational Linguistics circles, RST has been mainly used in natural language generation for content planning purposes, e.g. (Kosseim et al 2000), (Reed et al 1998). Besides this area, Marcu (Marcu 1997, 2000) developed a general framework and efficient strategies to recognize a number of major rhetorical structures in various kinds of texts. The main challenges are the recognition and delimitation of textual units and the identification of relations that hold between them. The rhetorical parsing algorithm he introduced relies on a first-order formalization of valid text structures which obey a number of structural assumptions. These, however, seem to be somewhat too restrictive. In particular our observations show that relations may occur between non-overlapping text spans; relations may also be either vertical or horizontal (they can involve non parent nodes). Text structure is a binary-branching tree in most cases, but a number of situations with more than two nodes have been observed in technical texts.

Marcu's work is based on a number of psycholinguistic investigations (Grosz et al. 1986) that show that discourse markers are used by human subjects both as cohesive links between adjacent clauses and as connectors between larger textual units. An important result is that discourse markers are used consistently with the semantics and pragmatics of the textual units they connect and they are relatively frequently used and non-ambiguous.

Investigating the Structure of Explanation

Corpus Analysis and Annotation

In order to identify explanation functions in technical texts and then in order to propose general explanation construction principles, a manual annotation of a portion of our corpus was carried out. This was realized on 74 different texts from our development corpus (about 88 pages), with the same training and annotation instructions given to several annotators. This is not a very large corpus because manual annotation is very much time consuming. Rules are then constructed manually by generalizing over classes of similar constructions found in the corpus. This situation does not require as many annotated instances as an automatic learning procedure would, whatever it may be. These rules and the lexical data used as linguistic cues are also extended in the generalization phase by the introduction of closely related terms or constructions.

Constructing a corpus in general is a very challenging task: it is first necessary to identify the parameters to measure, while keeping the others constant. Then, the scope of each parameter needs to be defined (the values they can take) and the value distributions (the percentage of texts for each parameter value which is needed for an adequate observation). The next step is the corpus construction, and its validation w.r.t. these parameters. Our parameters entail the taking into account of the following features:

- domains (energy, chemistry, transportation, food processing),
- authors (technical writers, engineers, administrative staff),
- type of style (basic, normal, elaborated with a rich typography),
- target audience (technicians from beginner to confirmed, engineers) and
- the difficulty to realize the procedure (i.e. complex temporal sequences of actions, use of complex equipment, large number of warnings).

The 74 selected texts allow us to make an indicative analysis that gives useful research directions and helps to establish and to confirm our working method.

The second step is the annotation. This is a difficult task: identifying and categorizing rhetorical relations is never straightforward. To help annotators, before any manual annotation, texts are automatically tagged with quite a good accuracy. This tagging includes the basic structures typical of procedures: titles, prerequisites, instructions, goal expressions, and various discourse markers (Delpech et al. 2008).

Annotators received the same training. After an adaptation period, needed for a comprehensive assimilation of the notions used in discourse analysis, annotators could realize a homogeneous task with a relatively good consensus of 86%, measured by a Kappa test. Training may be time consuming because notions in discourse analysis are less clear than in e.g. predicate-argument analysis. Training ends when there is little hesitation between discourse structure types when annotating technical texts.

Over the 74 texts, 1127 structures related to explanation have been annotated, i.e. about 15 annotations per text. Distribution over texts ranges from 3 to 28 depending on the length of the text but also on the domain and the target audience. We kept those annotations that occur at least 10 times over the whole set of texts, which corresponds to a frequency of about 1%. This sounds minimal level to us to be really of interest, in spite of the fact that some non-frequent structures may be of interest because they introduce interesting views on explanation structures.

We basically consider the following discourse structures, called hereafter ***Elementary Explanation Structures*** (EES). Definitions are informal, they follow from commonly admitted definitions that we have somewhat simplified considering that technical documents have structures of a moderate complexity:

- ***elaboration and evaluation***:

elaboration (adds new information),

illustration (provides related examples),

reformulation (simply restates, does not add any information),

result (specifies the outcome of an action),

contrast (introduces a comparison or a difference between two methods, objects or situations),

analogy (is a form of comparison to help understanding),

encouragement, hint, evaluation (explains a user what kind of result he should get so that he feels safe or can evaluate his performances).

- ***arguments:***

warning,

advice (very few threats or rewards, where the author is involved).

Arguments often have the form of a causal expression, informally: do X "because/otherwise" Z, with quite a large variety of causal marks (Fontan et al. 2008). X is usually called the conclusion (it is the action to carry out) and Z is the support of the conclusion in argumentation theory, it expresses the risks if the action is not realized fully and correctly.

- ***condition:*** involves at least two structures:

condition with the two branches then - else, the condition being in general introduced by "if" or "when".

assumption structure, which is an hypothetical statement.

- ***cause:*** involves a statement and an ensuing situation as defined in (Talmy 2001). We limit annotations to trans-sentential causal expressions, i.e. those operating over instructions.

- ***concession:*** a general rule is given followed by an exception that could be admitted.

- ***goal expression***: expresses purpose, following (Talmy 2001).

- ***frame:*** circumstances or restrictions on the context or the realization of an action, or expression of some forms of propositional attitudes such as: commitment, authority.

In a text, annotations corresponding to these tags can be embedded, leading to complex structures. In our corpus, annotations are in XML with attributes. This allows the encoding of e.g. the strength or weight of arguments, and meta-annotations such as the certainty of the annotator. A given structure may receive several annotations in case of ambiguity, overlap or conjunction of functions, this is expressed by the symbol “/” interpreted as the disjunction.

An example, in readable form, borrowed from didactics, is the following (to facilitate reading, most marks produced by the <TextCoop> system are omitted, only EES are given, instructions appear on new lines):

[$_{\text{procedure}}$
[$_{\text{purpose}}$ *Writing a paper:* [$_{\text{elaboration}}$ *Read light sources, then thorough]]*
[$_{\text{assumption/circumstance}}$ *Assuming you've been given a topic,]*
[$_{\text{circumstance}}$ *When you conduct research],*
move from light to thorough resources
[$_{\text{purpose}}$ *to make sure you're moving in the right direction].*
Begin by doing searches on the Internet about your topic
[$_{\text{purpose}}$ *to familiarize yourself with the basic issues;]*
[$_{\text{temporal-sequence}}$ *then] move to more thorough research on the Academic Databases;*
[$_{\text{temporal-sequence}}$ *finally], probe the depths of the issue by burying yourself in the library.*
[$_{\text{warning}}$ *Make sure that despite beginning on the Internet, you don't simply end there.*
[$_{\text{elaboration}}$ *A research paper using only Internet sources is a weak paper,*
[$_{\text{consequence}}$ *which puts you at a disadvantage...]]]*
[$_{\text{contrast}}$ *While the Internet should never be your only source of information, it would be ridiculous not to utilize its vast sources of information.]*
[$_{\text{advice}}$ *You should use the Internet to acquaint yourself with the topic more before you dig into more academic texts.]*

From these pages of annotated texts, we can induce more abstract regularities related to (1) the communicative goals specific to technical documents and (2) the way these goals are realized. For example, behind "advice" or "purpose" there is a communicative goal, respectively designed, within the context of technical documents, to help the user via a suggestion and to explain him the reasons of an action.

A General Analysis of Explanation Functions

From an analysis of the tagged corpus and considering how procedures are written and used by technicians or casual users, a first, global classification can be proposed of quite a large number of "conceptual" functions that realize the communicative goals required in procedures and in technical documents more generally. These are called ***explanation***

functions. To carry out this task, our strategy was to identify, categorize and structure the underlying communicative aims associated with the annotations or groups of annotations. This produces a second, more abstract level of annotations. Again, this is somewhat intuitive, but this was however realized as a collective task with the aim of reaching a consensus.

Here are the main categories and their organisation, which seem to be quite stable. To go deeper into more specialized explanation functions, it is obviously necessary to carry out further investigations, testing and refinements. It should be noted, and this is visible in our examples, that these functions apply to professional as well as to non-professional types of procedures.

We feel that these explanation functions and the linguistic means that characterize them can be used as guidelines as technical document guidelines. These functions are indeed simple and of an easy access to most readers.

Within an operational context in a broad sense, explanation functions can schematically be subdivided into two fields:

- the motivations for doing something ("Why do action A?") and
- the way to make something ("How-to do A?").

This view establishes a more global analysis of actions with the dichotomy intentions and motivations on the one hand and realization and its facets on the other hand, as can be found in Action Theory with a more philosophical view.

To avoid any confusion with EES names or with any existing term in RST, our explanation functions, which are abstract constructs, are prefixed by E-.

Let us now introduce these functions. These remain abstract at this level: their language realizations are accounted by schemes, illustrated in the next section. Examples in English are given here. We worked on French and English. We noted that classification results seem to be stable over these two languages (and probably also over a large number of languages). Linguistic realizations are often relatively similar.

Why do A?

The *why do A?* category of EES, the motivation functions, is basically organized in two subsets. The first subset, is composed of information providers: E-explicit, E-information. The second subset goes deeper into the action motivations and the potential risks. This subset is composed of a variety of arguments typical of technical texts: E-arguments.

The function **E-explicit** enhances or makes more explicit the structure of an action (or a set of actions) being carried out and its coherence w.r.t. related actions, usually found before or after the action at stake. It is in a large part composed of low-level goals or functions (*push the white button [to open the box]*), indicating the role of an instruction and the expected results. As confirmed by ergonomic investigations, goal expressions which have a limited scope appear in general at the end of the instruction. This function also includes several forms of structures dedicated to actions synchronization realized by means of temporal connectors, punctuation or typography. These marks make more explicit the macro-organization of instructions.

The aim of the **E-information** function, which operates at the ideational level, is to enhance, reinforce, weaken or contradict the beliefs of the reader, as anticipated by the author of the text. This is realized by providing more specific information on some aspects of the action at stake (*Adding salt to your sauce is unnecessary because fish sauce is already salted*).

Besides this very general function, two more accurate functions can be introduced, which convey information in a more neutral way w.r.t. the reader's beliefs: **E-clarification** (*Poke the wire into the bottom of the flower [(where the stem was)] as far as you can without it coming out the other side*) and **E-precision** (*Hang the hanger in a dark area and wait for the flowers to dry. [A full drying process will take between 2 and 3 weeks.]*).

The second subset of this group operates at the inter-personal level, and aims at motivating the user to realize the action at stake as required and as accurately as possible, following precautions and recommendations. This subset is composed of various types of arguments, usually found in argumentation classifications: **E-warnings** (*Carefully plug in the mother card vertically otherwise you risk to damage its connectors*) and **E-advice** (*We recommend professional products for your leathers, they will offer a stronger protection while repairing some minor damages*), when there is no implication on the author's part. Conversely, there is an implication of the author or his institution in **E-threats** (*You must confirm your connection within 30 minutes otherwise we will cancel it*) and **E-rewards** (*We suggest you to pay when you book your flight since a discount coupon will be offered for your next purchase*) otherwise. These functions are designed to justify the importance of an action and to anticipate potential problems by stressing on the necessity of doing it as required (warnings). Another option is to indicate the optional character of an action (advice) and the benefits of doing it. Besides the recognition of arguments, evaluating their illocutionary or persuasion strength is of much interest. This is realized in general via a series of marks, essentially adverbial, denoting various levels of intensity.

How to do A?

This second category of functions develops the way to realize an action, the *How-to-do A?* functions. It contains several EES families. The first one deals with functions related to controls on the user actions, while the second family is related to the control of his interpretations. The third family includes help functions.

In the first family, control on user actions, an important function is **E-guidance**. This function has quite fuzzy boundaries, it can simply include temporal marks guiding the organization of actions (similarly to E-Structure). It can also include manners, durations and a variety of information on instruments, equipment and products to use. This allows the introduction of a number of details on how to realize and coordinate actions (*Open the box: use a 2.5 inch key and a screw-driver*). These are related to the argument structure of the action verb of the main part of the instruction. They are however analysed as adjuncts.

The next function in this family, **E-framing**, indicates, via a statement often starting a sentence or a paragraph, the context of application of an instruction or of a group of instructions (*[for X25-01 pumps]: disable first...*). To be more visible, this function may also be realized as a low level title. Next, **E-expected-result** describes the target result. It is a means for the user to evaluate his performances and to make sure he is on the right track (*at this stage, the liquid must be dark brown*). Finally, **E-elaboration** explains in more depth how to realize an action (*Hold the seedling by the stem with your palm facing the roots of the plant, and turn the soda bottle upside down, [lightly shaking the soil out and the plant with it]*). It may also be viewed as a kind of zoom over a subset of actions, to make sure the user understand how to realize the action.

The second family is related to the control of the interpretations made by the user. The goal is to make sure he correctly understands the text. In this class fall relatively well-known functions directly associated with rhetorical relations: **E-definition** gives a definition of a certain concept in order to make sure the reader has a good knowledge of that concept (*The transmission in your car is a gearbox that transmits powers from the engine to the live axle*). **E-reformulation** says the same thing with different words or constructions, there is no new informational contents, (*Before starting, make sure you have the right experience and skills, in* *other words that you can do the job*). **E-illustration** gives one or more relevant examples in relation with the task to realize.

The third family is composed of two functions which provide basic help to the user: **E-encouragements** supports in some way the user attention and efforts, (*at this stage, the most difficult operations have been realized*). **E-evaluation** provides a precise evaluation of what should be observed at this point so that the user can check if he did well or not, (*If the paste is really crunchy, then you are an excellent cook, you can move on to the next step*).

These functions can be organized by groups leading to explanation plans, e.g. make sure the task is correctly understood (E-definition, E-reformulation) and then warn about risks (E-warning). Planning explanation is the ultimate goal of an author of technical documents while taking into account the prototypical profile of his readers.

Explanation Schemes

Explanation schemes deal with the level of language realizations of explanation functions. Explanation schemes are structured sequences of EES. These schemes are defined from corpus analysis by associating sequences of EES annotations with a manual identification of explanation functions. This approach is somewhat intuitive, however explanation functions which have been identified by this method have been recognized as relevant and realistic by technical writers. Examples of explanation schemes are often found in authoring recommendations proper to companies. Generalizing over language structures associated with a given explanation function allows stable definitions for the main explanation schemes found in technical texts. This also allows the description of a grammar for each explanation function. This grammar is based on EES possibly associated with constrained statements. In the Dislog formalism, the EES are pre-terminal elements, while explanation functions are non-terminal symbols which may enter into other schemes. An explanation scheme may occur in several explanation functions.

Most explanation functions may be organized in a large diversity of ways, using EES in different manners. However, since technical documents follow in general quite precise authoring guidelines, as presented in Chapter 3, only a small number of forms are really recurrent. In general, explanation functions are short, with a maximum of three EES. Beyond the use of three EES, it is often admitted that the instruction which is given is not sufficiently clear and must probably be rewritten. When a substantial set of explanation is necessary, then an elaboration must be produced, which is, in our view, a kind of sub-procedure or a zoom on a specific subtask.

As an illustration, a number of very recurrent and prototypical explanation schemes associated with explanation are given below. These schemes are given here in standard bracketed notation, each bracketed term corresponding to an EES. In our notation, the * indicates multiple occurrences. There are obviously many other schemes which may depend on authoring guidelines or on technical writer practices. However, the principles and the approach remain the same for the various situations and corpora we have analysed.

The E-warning scheme has the general structure:

E-warning → [warning_conclusion] / [[warning_conclusion] [warning_support]*] /
[[warning] [illustration]*] /
[[warning] [illustration]* [elaboration]*] /
[[circumstance]* [warning]] /
[[circumstance]* [warning_conclusion] [warning_support]*]

These schemes indicate that an E-warning is composed of the following EES: either a warning alone or with its support(s), a warning followed by one or more illustrations, or a warning followed by one or more illustrations and elaborations. Finally, specific circumstances may limit the range of a warning.

The E-advice explanation scheme is defined in a similar way:

E-advice → [advice_conclusion] /
[[advice_conclusion] [advice_support]*] /
[[advice] [illustration]*] /
[[circumstance]* [advice]] /
[[circumstance]* [advice_conclusion] [advice_support]*]

E-definition, E-illustration and E-expected-result have the general following structure:

E-definition → [[definition] [illustration]*]
E-illustration → [illustration]* / [[circumstance] [illustration]*]
E-expected-result → [[circumstance]
[statement expr(+modal, +necessity)]]

This latter example requires a statement with a modal expression such as "must" which introduces a kind of necessity (e.g. *at this stage, the engine must be cold).*

Explanation functions can be complex compounds and may include other explanation functions, e.g.:

E-warning → [[$_{\text{warning}}$] E-illustration*]
which refers to an EES followed by another explanation function.

E-explicit can be realized in a number of ways since an instruction or a related piece of information can be made more precise in different manners depending on what exactly needs to be made more explicit, e.g. a manner, an equipment type. The most frequent forms encountered in technical texts at the discourse level are based on illustrations, reformulations, definitions or the decomposition of an instruction into a sequence of instructions with conditions or circumstances. E-explicit can therefore have the following forms:

E-explicit → [$_{\text{illustration}}$] /
[$_{\text{reformulation}}$] /
[[$_{\text{condition}}$] [$_{\text{instruction}}$]]* /
[[$_{\text{circumstance}}$] [$_{\text{instruction}}$]]* /
E-definition / E-elaboration.

E-clarification is more restricted. It is essentially based on providing illustrations or definitions. E-precision is often realized at the level of the arguments of the instruction main verb, by using e.g. a reformulation or an illustration.

E-clarification → [$_{\text{illustration}}$] /
[$_{\text{definition}}$] .

E-framing basically introduces a circumstance or a condition that has scope over several instructions. Warnings and advice can also appear within the scope of E-framing. The main role of this explanation function is to restrict the use of these instructions to a certain context:

E-framing → [$_{\text{circumstance}}$] [$_{\text{instructions}}$]*
[$_{\text{condition}}$] [$_{\text{instructions}}$]*.

E-guidance decomposes an instructions which may be felt to be too complex or too general into a few instructions with application conditions or specific circumstances. Specific warnings or advice may be included, but they are not as central as conditions or circumstances. E-guidance has essentially the following structure:

E-guidance → [[$_{\text{condition}}$] [$_{\text{instruction}}$]]* /
[[$_{\text{circumstance}}$] [$_{\text{instruction}}$]]*.

Explanation functions such as E-definition, E-encouragement or E-evaluation have a more shallow discourse structure. They may contain EES, but they are in a large part composed of text which cannot be solely reduced to the types of discourse structures given above. Indeed, for example, a definition describes by means of features (functions or parts) an object, an instrument or a product.

Besides explanation strictly speaking, discourse constraints are often imposed on the structure of instructions. For example, an instruction must:

- always start by the main clause, with the verb first, then conditions of application follow, or
- always start with the context or conditions of application, then the instruction and, finally, the justifications, if any.

Another consideration is that instructions rarely come in isolation in a sentence, unless the actions to carry out are very simple or the user is assumed to have difficulties to realize the task. Instructions are often conjoined in a single sentence and come by small groups which are closely related. Consider e.g.:

Carefully open the telephone box, remove the dust in it and leave a mark.

It would sound awkward to decompose this small group of instructions into three sentences, since they share the same object and probably a manner. We call this form of very natural grouping an ***instructional compound***. All the construction principles given above for instructions also apply to instructional compounds.

The Linguistic Structure of Elementary Explanation Structures (EES)

General Considerations

Let us now consider the linguistic structure of EES, and let us first consider how the description of EES is organized and how they can form larger structures. For that purpose, it is recommended to proceed in a modular way, describing each discourse structure separately, to make descriptions more modular. It is also crucial to be able to test patterns or rules independently from each other.

Next, given a set of rules for an EES, tests must be realized to evaluate recognition accuracy and also the interactions between rules. Finally, given a set of EES, it is important to manage the way and the order the different EES are recognized and tagged in a text since there may exist recognition conflicts. Then, on the basis of selective binding rules, those elementary structures can be bound to form larger structures.

The language Dislog, presented in Chapter 4, is designed to manage a variety of constraints in a declarative way that can manage constraints, conflicts and various forms of binding.

Discourse analysis, and the analysis of the structure of explanation in particular, is quite a difficult task. Our approach is organized as follows:

- The structure of nuclei and satellites of the different relations is first defined, focussing on their fundamental structure, something comparable to a base form in sentence syntax.
- Next the lexical resources which are needed are developed and categorized (connectors, verb classes, some types of adverbs, etc.), the lexical entries are enriched from the data which is observed in corpora,
- The additional linguistic resources which are needed are then developed, e.g.: morphology, punctuation, aspect,
- Finally binding principles are developed together with various types of constraints (e.g. non overlap) when appropriate.

Each of the above four systems is relatively simple and modular; it captures interesting linguistic observations and generalizations. The complexity arises from the interactions between these systems.

The binding principles defined in Dislog must be able to detect complex constructions and combinations of EES. The following situations have been observed:

- several EES structures may be embedded,
- EES structures may be chained (when a satellite is a nucleus for another relation),
- nuclei and related satellites may be non-adjacent,
- nuclei may be linked to several satellites of different types,
- some satellites may be embedded into their nucleus.

As a result, discourse relations taken in isolation receive a relatively simple description, with well-identified lexical resources. The mechanisms implemented in <TextCoop> manage the hard recognition tasks, including binding these structures, under well-formedness constraints.

As shall be seen below, resources needed to recognize EES are essentially lexical, e.g.: connectors, verbs, semantic features. A few grammatical and morphological considerations are also used. This limited number of resources makes discourse analysis relatively re-usable in various application domains and in various textual genres.

Another observation is that it is much easier to recognize satellites than nuclei, which, in the case of explanation, are quite neutral from the language point of view. In a number of situations, it is necessary to develop inferences based on knowledge to be able to accurately identify a nucleus. A prototypical example is developed below for illustrations. While the satellite is clearly marked, the nucleus can only be identified on the basis of domain or general purpose knowledge.

From a foundational point of view, our analysis of discourse and explanation aims at defining a kind of conceptual or cognitive analysis of discourse: besides text spans involved in discourse relation which convey a certain meaning, it is also of much interest to precisely identify the semantics conveyed by the relations themselves. This consideration involves the taking into account syntactic considerations such as the position of the various text spans, following e.g. the principles of Construction Grammars for sentence syntax.

The Dislog Rule Formalism

Dislog and <TextCoop> are presented in detail in Chapter 4. Let us present here the basic elements of Dislog to facilitate the understanding of the rules given in the next sections.

The formalism adopted in Dislog extends the BNF format. A rule in Dislog has the following general form:

L(Representation) --> R, {P}.

where:

- L is a non-terminal symbol.
- Representation is the representation resulting from the analysis
- R is a sequence of symbols as described below, and
- P is a set of predicates and functions implemented in Prolog that realize the various computations and controls, and that allow the inclusion of inference and knowledge into rules. These are not addressed in this chapter.

R is a finite sequence of the following elements:

- ***terminal symbols*** that represent words, expressions, punctuations, html and XML tags. Terminal symbols are included between square brackets,
- ***preterminal symbols***: are symbols which are derived directly into terminal elements. These are used to capture various forms of generalizations, facilitating rule authoring and update. Symbols can be associated with a set of arguments (as in any Prolog clause) or, preferably, a type feature structure that encodes a variety of aspects of those symbols, from morphology to semantics,
- ***non-terminal symbols***, which can also be associated with type feature structures. These symbols refer to "local grammars", i.e. grammars that encode specific syntactic constructions such as temporal

expressions or domain specific constructs. Non-terminal symbols do not include discourse structure symbols: Dislog rules cannot call each other, this feature is dealt with by the selective binding principle, which constructs discourse structures,
- ***optionality and iteration marks*** over non-terminal and preterminal symbols, as in regular expressions, these are noted with the curly brackets and the star respectively,
- ***gaps***, which are symbols that stand for a finite sequence of words of no present interest for the rule which must be skipped. A gap can appear only between terminal, preterminal or non-terminal symbols. Dislog offers the possibility to specify in a gap a list of elements which must not be skipped: when such an element is found before the termination of the gap, then the gap fails. The length of the string that is skipped can also be controlled. For that purpose, a ***skip*** predicate is also included in the language: it is close to a gap and simply allows the parser to skip a maximum number of words given as a parameter.

A Repository of Rules and Lexical Resources

The following rules and lexical data have been designed for French and English. The structures presented here are those frequently or relatively frequently encountered in technical texts in English. These structures have in general much more diverse forms and uses in general language, as developed in e.g. (Marcu 1997) and (Marcu 2000). We present here samples of rules and lexical resources for English required for procedural text processing. These rules may seem simplistic or unrealistic compared to the structures which are usually found in general language. But they do correspond to what has been observed over a large diversity of texts. One of the reasons is that technical texts are restricted forms of language where the different discourse articulations must be as simple and direct as possible.

The way the rules given below are implemented and developed is given in Chapter 5. The goal of this section is not to give a comprehensive grammar for rules required for technical document processing, but rather to illustrate the main structures and how they can be defined, formulated and implemented using a limited number of linguistic resources. We introduce in this chapter a method that readers can use and enhance for processing a variety of technical texts.

In this section, we present most of the structures found in procedural texts and in requirements. Technical documents may also contain structures such as definitions. We present here titles, instructions, advice and warnings conclusions (kernels) and advice and warnings supports (satellites). Samples of binding rules are given for advice and warnings to show how elementary structures are bound to form larger ones. This process is recursive. Instructions can be analysed as satellites for titles. Subtitles can also be analysed as satellites to the main title, which is the root of the documents. Its role is to express the main goal of the procedure. Similarly, prerequisites, summaries or preliminaries can be analysed as satellites to the main title. These structures are not developed here: they are quite peripheral and essentially based on typography.

We focus on a number of frequently encountered satellite structures: cause, condition, concession, contrast, circumstance, purpose, illustration and restatement. As illustrated in Chapters 4 and 5, identifying the kernels of these satellites is often quite challenging because they are rarely clearly linguistically marked. Knowledge is often required to identify them and to resolve ambiguities.

Structures such as definitions or encouragements are not presented here because they have general text structures. Definition structures have been explored in e.g. the TREC project and in the Semantic Web.

Designing EES rules has entailed the definition of a number of dedicated lexical item categories. More generic information can be found in (Taboada 2006) who has developed a relatively large analysis of the distribution of linguistic marks in various discourse structures. Restricted to technical documents, we have the following sets of marks:

- connectors and related elements, which are organized by general types: time, cause, concession, etc. An interesting and recent analysis of the role of connectors in discourse analysis is reported in e.g. (Stede 2012),
- terms which are specific to certain discourse functions,
- verbs organized by semantic classes, close to those found in WordNet, that have been adapted or refined for discourse analysis, e.g. propositional attitude verbs or report verbs (Wierzbicka, 1987),
- terms with positive or negative polarity, in particular for warnings and advice.

The following subsections provide rule examples, which are among the most common and the most simple. For the sake of readability, some minor simplifications have been introduced in the symbol specifications. The rule base is available on demand.

For each discourse relation, a definition is given in addition to the rule sample and the related resources. In the rules, *bos* stands for beginning of sentence or structure, while *eos* stands for end of sentence or end of segment. The end of a segment can be characterized by a typographic mark such as the end of an enumeration element or a connector introducing a new structure. In the rules, the curly brackets indicate that an element is optional. Resources given here are in general just samples of the most prototypical elements, not the comprehensive set.

Instructions

An instruction is a proposition, often in an injunctive form, that expresses an elementary action (*open the box, fill in the tank, check the APU*). The proposition that describes the action may contain various elements such as instruments, equipment, manners, whose aim is to be as explicit as possible on the way the action must be realized. Subordinate clauses can be included in instructions to express restrictions.

The subject of the main proposition is often left implicit because it designates the operator doing the action. The main verb of an instruction is an action verb (*close, clean*) or an epistemic verb (*control, memorize*), it denotes the action to realize. The verb is often in the imperative or infinitive form. Finite forms may however appear in non-professional documents such as video games solutions or cooking recipes where the tone is more familiar.

Finally, an instruction does not a priori contain any negation, however, there are cases where it cannot be avoided (see Chapter 3). Negations basically characterize warnings which are developed below (*Never smoke while filling in the tank, do not eat while dismounting* ...).

The beginning of an instruction is often the start of the corresponding sentence. It can be introduced by various typographic marks proper to enumerations, e.g. intended lines, bullets etc., which occur in about 77% of the situations we observed (Luc et al, 1999). These marks also indicate the beginning of an instruction. The end of an instruction is either a punctuation mark, usually the dot, sometimes the semicolon or the comma, a connector, or typographic marks introducing the next instruction, these are often implicit temporal marks.

Within an instruction, the action is in general organized around the action verb and its arguments. Goals, references, manners, limits, are all adjuncts which appear in various orders. Goals contain specific verbs while manners are often nominal. The type of verbs encountered in procedures is quite different from those found in ordinary texts. We compared our procedures with standard books and observed the following distributions. For procedures we have:

(1) factive verb: 67%

(2) stative verb: 18%

(3) declarative verb: 15% and
(4) no performative verb,

while we have for non-procedural texts:

(1) factive verb: 41%
(2) stative verb: 35%
(3) declarative verb: 23% and
(4) performative verb: 1%.

It is then quite simple to identify among texts those which are procedural by taking into account the typography, which is very rich in procedures and the verb distribution. The main structures for instructions are the following:

Instruction →
bos, gap(neg), verb(action, infinitive), gap, eos. /
bos, gap(neg), verb(light), gap, verb(action, infinitive), gap, eos.

Where infinitive denotes a verb in the infinitive form (without "to"), light indicates a light verb, neg represents the negation, and action denotes an action verb, which is in general domain dependent. The two rules above require that there is no negation before the verb, this is noted as gap(neg).

Besides modals and a few terms like pronouns, the main resource which is necessary to recognize instructions is a list of action verbs. This list is in general very large, more than 10 000 terms. However, in most cases, there is a need for only a limited set of verbs, e.g. about 100.

Titles

Titles introduce a document or a part of it. In our context they express a high level goal. The instructions and the explanation elements that follow a title describe a way to reach the corresponding goal. Subtitles introduce a goal sub-goal hierarchy.

The recognition of titles is a specific problem. It can be implemented based on the typography of the document if there are dedicated marks (e.g. in html or XML or section numbers). Title identification in procedures is developed in (Delpech et al. 2008). Title analysis raises two main problems:

-The identification of the title hierarchy, for which domain knowledge is often required. For example, in: *making a pizza: the paste…, the topping…* unless it is known that a pizza is composed of these two elements that require a separate preparation, it is difficult to say e.g. that the topping is a subtitle of a level equivalent to the paste or whether it is a higher level title, comparable to making a pizza. The typography used in procedures is not necessarily rich enough to raise this ambiguity.

-The "reconstruction" of the full meaning of a title. Titles are indeed often elliptic: they are often formed of a noun phrase which is the object of the proposition (e.g. above: *the topping* standing for *preparing the topping*) or a verb, possibly in gerund form, without any complement (e.g. *cleaning, assembling*).

In general the structure of titles is very similar to the structure of instructions. They are however shorter and the verb they include is in general relatively generic.

Advice

An advice is a type of argument. It is a complex structure that often involves a relation between a conclusion and a support. The conclusion invites the reader to perform an optional action to obtain better results, and the support gives the motivations and the expected benefits. The support is not necessarily explicit since it may be obvious to the reader.

Advice structures are organized around terms that express notions such as an optional action, a preference or a choice. The main structures for the conclusion are the following:

Advice_conclusion →
verb(preference, infinitive), gap(G), eos. /
[it,is], {adv_prob}, gap, exp(advice1), gap, eos. /
exp(advice2), [:], gap, eos.

With:
verb(preference): choose, prefer
exp(advice1): a good idea, better, recommended, preferable,
exp(advice2): a tip, an advice, best option, alternative,
adv_prob: probably, possibly, etc.

The following structures are recognized as advice:

Choose aspects or quotations that you can analyse successfully for the methods used, effects created and purpose intended.

Following your thesis statement, it is a good idea to add a little more detail that acts to preview each of the major points that you will cover in the body of the essay.

A useful tip: open each paragraph with a topic sentence.

The support of an advice gives the reasons for acting as suggested. Basically, advice supports have one of the three following forms:

(1) Advice_support → goal_exp, {adverb}, positively oriented term, gap, eos.

Goal exp includes e.g.: *in order to, for, whereas*, adverb includes: *better, optimal*, etc. and positively oriented term includes: nouns (*savings, perfection, gain*, etc.), adjectives (*efficient, easy, useful*, etc.), or adverbs (*well, simply,* etc.).

(2) Advice_support → pronoun, gap, verb(positive_consequence), gap, eos.

A verb with a positive consequence may be a favor verb (*favor, encourage, save,* etc.) or a facilitation verb (*improve, optimize, facilitate, embellish, help, contribute,* etc.),

(3) Advice_support → pronoun, gap, aux(future), expr(positive_consequence), gap, eos.

A recognized structure is, for example: *it will be easier to locate your keys.*

Advice supports are bound to their related conclusion by means of binding rules. Supports may either precede or follow the conclusion. The following example shows how an XML annotation allows the identification of these two structures:

<Argument>
<Advice_conclusion> you should better let a 10 cm interval between the wall and the lattice, </Advice_conclusion >

<Advice_support> this space will allow the air to move around, which is beneficial for the health of your plant. </Advice_support>
</Argument>

Warnings

A warning is a type of instruction that needs to be realized with great care because of direct or indirect risks that the user or the equipment that is manipulated may undergo (e.g. in technical documents: health problems, equipment damages, pollution).

Similarly to advice structures, a warning is composed of a conclusion (the action) and one or more support(s) which describe the risks or the potential problems. Several types of very injunctive expressions and possibly typical forms of typography or icons are often used.

The main warning structures are the following:

Warning_conclusion →
exp(ensure), gap(G), eos. /
[it,is], {adv(intensity)}, adj(imp), gap(G),
verb(action, infinitive), gap(G), eos.

Resources:
exp(ensure): ensure, make sure, be sure
adv(intensity): very, absolutely, really
adj(imp): essential, vital, crucial, fundamental

The following utterances are typical warnings:
Make sure your facts are relevant rather than related.
It is essential that you follow the guidelines for each pipe as set by the manual.

Supports convey negative statements, the following four main structures have been identified, they are characterized by various types of marks:

(1) Warning_support --> connector(cause), gap, expr(negative), gap, eos.

Connectors include: *because, otherwise*, negative expressions include verbs expressing a negative consequence or negative expressions (*injuries, overload, pain,* etc.),

(2) Warning_support --> connector(negative), gap, eos.

These supports are formed with negative connectors such as: *in order not to, in order to avoid, under the risk of, etc.*

(3) Warning_support --> connector(cause), gap, verb(risk), gap, eos.

These supports are constructed with specific verbs such as risk verbs introducing an event: *you risk to break*,

(4) More generally, expressions with very negative terms, such as: nouns: *death, disease, etc.*, adjectives: *unwanted, dangerous*, and some verbs and adverbs.

Binding rules for advice and warnings

Warning conclusions and supports which are related must be bound. The same situation holds for advice. This is realized by means of selective binding rules. These rules are used to construct discourse structures from EES. These are presented in Chapter 4. They have a syntax similar to discourse structure rules. The marks they use are however essentially based on XML tags.

Here is a simple example of a binding rule. Warnings are composed of a conclusion and a support. These two structures are recognized separately by dedicated rules as shown above.

Let us assume that both warning supports and conclusions are explicitly tagged, then, a simple binding rule is:

Warning →
<warning-concl>,gap(G1),</warning-concl>, gap(G2),

<warning-supp>, gap(G1), </warning-supp>, gap(G3), eos.

Then, the whole structure is tagged by e.g. <warning>:

<Argument>
<Warning_conclusion> Carefully plug-in the mother card vertically </Warning_conclusion>
<Warning_support> otherwise you risk to damage its connectors. </Warning_support>
</Argument>

The same rule can be defined for advice constructions to bind a conclusion with a support. Rules binding a conclusion with several supports are defined in a similar way, e.g. to handle cases such as:

To clean leather armchairs choose specialized products dedicated to furniture, and prefer them colorless, [*they will play a protection role, add beauty, and repair some small damages*] which contains three supports given between square brackets.

Similar rules are defined to bind any kind of nucleus with their related satellites, adjacent of non-adjacent. In case of non-adjacency, the problem of structure relatedness must be investigated.

Cause

Cause, as found in procedural discourse, has a relatively simple linguistic structure. This is, by far, not the case in general language. It is a relation where a segment, traditionally called the antecedent, provokes the realization of an event (the consequent). The antecedent and the consequent are linked by a causal connector, usually *because* or related forms. However, the comma may also be an implicit connector.

Two very simple rules are the following:

Cause →
conn(cause), gap(G), ponct(comma). /
conn(cause), gap(G), eos.

The lexical resources are:

conn(cause): because, because of, on account of
ponct(comma): , ; :

In the following examples, note that the consequent may appear before the antecedent:

Because books are so thorough and long, you have to learn to skim.
Long lists result in shallow essays because you don't have space to fully explore an idea.
Many poorly crafted essays have been produced on account of a lack of preparation and confidence.

At a clause level, verbs expressing consequence or cause such as *entail, provoke, imply* are also frequently encountered.

We will not investigate very much this structure here since it has in general very simple manifestations in technical documents. (Talmy 2001) presents an in-depth investigation of different types of causal relations. Talmy refers to these as “lexicalization patterns”. Although this term may not be fully appropriate, those patterns give a good indication of the form of causal relations and of a number of distinctions on agentivity and the type of the resulting event. This is of interest in technical documents, e.g. resulting-event causation: *The vase broke from a ball’s rolling into it.,* causing-event causation: *A ball’s rolling into it broke the vase,* instrument causation: *A ball broke the vase, etc.* Besides Talmy, Dixon (2000), on the basis of a typology of causatives, discusses the syntax and semantics of a large number of types of causative constructions with great detail.

Conditions

A condition included in an instruction, or ranging over a set of instructions, specifies a situation which must be met for the instruction to be relevant and realized. A condition, in other words, sets the cases where an instruction must be executed. A condition in procedures is usually introduced by *if*, or possibly by *when* in case of a temporal dimension, or by *for*.

Condition →
conn(cond), gap(G), ponct(comma). /
conn(cond), gap(G), eos.

With the following lexical entries:

conn(cond): if, when, for

The following examples are recognized by the above rules:

If all of the sources seem to be written by the same person or group of people, you must again seriously consider the validity of the topic.

For first conclusions, don't be afraid to be short if you feel there is still an issue to resolve or a control to make.

Increase the voltage by 10 volts increments if the probe temperature drops below 100 degrees C.

Conditional expressions such as *assuming, in case, supposing, unless,* etc. are not frequently used in technical documents because of their hypothetical connotation or because they express a negative constraint, which is more difficult to handle than a positive one (e.g. *unless otherwise specified*). Conditional expression analysis is investigated in the literature from various points of view, formal of empirical. A very detailed analysis of conditionals in language and from a logical point of view can be found in (Declerk et al. 2001).

Concession

Concession is a relation between two text segments A and B where the segment B contradicts at least partly the segment A, or contradicts an implicit conclusion which can be drawn from segment A. Concessions have motivated a number of foundational investigations in formal linguistics (e.g. (Couper-Kuhlen et al. 2000)). Concessions are often categorized as denied phenomenal cause or motivational cause (or denied motive for doing something). These are quite complex to interpret in technical documents since the boundaries of what is allowed or not are not very clear. However, concessions can be a powerful means to summarize a situation.

The main rules are the following:

Concession →
conn(opposition_alth), gap(G1), ponct(comma), gap(G2), eos. /
conn(opposition_alth), gap(G), eos. /
conn(opposition_how), gap(G), eos.

With the following resources:

conn(opposition_alth): although, though, even though, even if, notwithstanding, despite, in spite of,

conn(opposition_how): however

Concessions may be found in an advice situation, as in the following example, or to express an exceptional situation, segments A and B are given together here:

Your paper should expose some new idea or insight about the topic, not just be a collage of other scholars' thoughts and research -- although you will definitely rely upon these scholars as you move toward your point.

The probe maximal temperature must not exceed 123 degrees, however, a temperature of up to 127 degrees is possible but for less than 30 seconds.

Contrast

Contrast is a major rhetorical relation, it is used very frequently. A contrast is a kind of symmetric relation between two segments A and B, where one segment is opposed in a certain way to the other. Typically, both clauses refer to a unique situation but imply a kind of contradiction. This apparent contradiction motivated the use of a defeasible inference logic and semantics, possibly using world knowledge to preserve the coherence of the whole structure. Contrast is typically introduced by the connectors *however, although* and *but.* Closely related relations are antithesis and concession (defined above). Of interest are e.g. the works of (Lakoff 1971), (Wolf and Gibson 2005) and (Spenader and Lobanova 2007), the latter develops an analysis of the differences between concession and contrast.

In traditional linguistic analysis, contrast is analysed as a denial of expectation, which is quite a strong view of this relation. For example in:

It is raining but I am taking an umbrella (Lakoff 1971) one can understand that the speaker is going to be wet, but taking an umbrella will contradict this initial expectation. Most investigations on contrast have concentrated on the analysis of the semantic relationships that could characterize such a notion and the situations which are related.

In technical documents, the uses of these relations are restricted to a few situations where the second part of the discourse relation is less central than the first one and introduces a form of comment, a preference or an exceptional situation which is not in a full contradiction with the first part of the statement. This second part is however very useful to the understanding of the action to realize.

The main rules for segment B are the following:

```
Contrast →
conn(opposition_whe), gap(G), ponct(comma). /
conn(opposition_whe), gap(G), eos. /
conn(opposition_how), gap(G), eos.
```

Resources are essentially:

conn(oppositio_whe): whereas, but whereas, however, although, but, while

Typical examples are (segment B following or preceding segment A):

The code is optimized for a 8-core CPU, but in general it will not be used on such machines.

Although they are not very handy for precision tasks, gloves D556 must be used to manipulate S34 probes when they are warm.

A key of type RD must be used to open the pipe, however, in case of emergency any immediately available key must be used.

The product is ready for use however, users need to activate their accounts by doing first time login…

Circumstance

Circumstance is a relation where the segment B introduces a kind of frame in which A occurs. Therefore, A is valid or must be realized according to the circumstances stated in B. B often appears before A. It is sometimes analysed as a subordinate clause. Circumstances are very diverse in form and contents: they may be temporal, spatial, related to particular events or occasions. In procedures, they describe or introduce specific situations, these may be syntactically close to conditionals, but play a different role. The main issue in the grammatical analysis of B is to describe the context in which A must be realized.

The main structures for Circumstance are:

Circumstance →
conn(circ), gap(G), ponct(comma). /
conn(circ), gap(G), eos.

Lexical resources are quite diverse, the most frequently encountered are in particular:

conn(circ): when, once, as soon as, after, before, in case of

A few typical examples are:

Before you put you start the truck engine, evaluate its trajectory.

Once the tank is empty, make sure it does not contain any trace of pesticide.

In case of frost, unlock the pipe security valve…

Purpose

Purpose is a relation where a segment B provides the motivation behind the action expressed in segment A. In general language, this relation has a large number of language realizations, uses and facets. In technical documents it is in general restricted to the expression of direct motivations and goals. When the segment B appears before the main clause of a sentence, it may have a wider scope than just this sentence: it may range over a few instructions following the sentence in which it appears. When B appears at the end of a sentence, its scope is in general restricted to the sentence in which it appears.

In technical documents, a purpose helps the operator to understand the role of the instruction or groups of instructions. This may be useful to make sure that the instruction(s) are properly understood and executed.

The main rules describing the structure of purposes within technical documents are the following:

Purpose →
conn(purpose), verb(action, infinitive), gap(G), ponct(comma). /
conn(purpose), verb(action, infinitive), gap(G), eos.

With, in particular:

conn(purpose): to, in order to, so as to

A few typical examples are:

Use an X38 key to close the tank.

To reschedule the process, launch the application...
In order to make the best of a writing assignment, there are a few rules that must always be followed.

Illustration

Illustration is a relation where segment B instantiates a segment A, or a part of it, by means of one or more elements, used as a representative sample for the class of objects, entities or events referred to by segment A. Illustration is a relatively simple notion, conceptually speaking, it is however realized by a large diversity of means, including punctuation and typography.

The structures typical of illustration are presented below:
Illustration →
exp(illus_eg), gap(G), eos. /
[here], auxiliary(be), gap(G1), exp(illus_exa), gap(G2), eos. /
[let,us,take], gap(G), exp(illus_bwe), eos.
With, for example, the following resources:
exp(illus_eg): e.g., including, such as
exp(illus_exa): example, an example, examples
exp(illus_bwe): by way of example, by way of illustration.
The following examples are recognized as illustrations:
This is a crucial point for other types of oil such as A35 and A37 lubs.
Here are some examples of how they can be used appropriately, so long as they are relevant to the task: ...
Prepare pizza toppings (e.g. tomato sauce, peperoni, eggs, mushrooms, etc.) separately.

Restatement

A restatement is a relation where segment B rephrases segment A without adding any new information. The goal is to make sure the instruction that is given is clear enough. A restatement is therefore simpler than an illustration or an elaboration, which adds new information.

A typical rule is the following:
Restatement →
ponct(opening_parenthesis),exp(restate),gap(G),
ponct(closing_parenthesis). /
exp(restate), gap(G), eos.
The main lexical resources are:
exp(restate): in other words, to put it another way, that is to say, i.e., put differently.

An example is:
Care not to close the aircraft main door when the APU is under test, in other words make sure the main door remains open.

Elaboration

Elaborations are also widely used in technical documents. Their role is to develop an action or an instruction that is felt to be complex and that needs to be explained in more depth in order to make sure that users can safely realize it. In our view, elaboration is a kind of proto- or meta-relation that includes more primitive relations such as those presented above. An elaboration can be viewed as a zoom over one or more instructions that has the form of a procedure. It is a structured set of more primitive relations that often undergo some form of planning.

According to a number of authors, elaboration refers to a group of discourse relations that connect utterances describing the same state of affairs. However, besides this general and quite fuzzy view, no in-depth concrete investigation on the elaboration relation have been carried out to the best of our knowledge.

In the context of technical documents, an elaboration contains sequences of instructions, warnings, advice, causes and motivations. An elaboration is a kind of micro-procedure, which is difficult to identify as an isolated structure, unless its right and left boundaries can be identified by e.g. a subtitle, a new paragraph or a topic change.

A Few Illustrations

The following text extracts are short illustrations of the above rules, applied on procedures. Different domains are presented, with short examples since outputs from long texts would be difficult to read. The output of our system is given here with some editing to facilitate reading. Note how structures are embedded, e.g. how conditions or circumstances are embedded into instructions.

<procedure>

<title> Installing panels on a flat roof </title>.

<warning> <warning-concl> Check with a level for any pitch or slope; even flat roofs often are framed with a slight angle to allow for drainage </ warning-concl></warning> .

<instruction> <verb type = action > Leave </verb> a 1 / 8 - inch gap between the panels <purpose> to allow for expansion </purpose> </instruction> .

etc.

</procedure>.

Examples from the gardening domain:

<instruction> By using peat based <verb type = action > plant </verb> -starting supplies (<illustration> such as peat pots , peat pellets or compressed peat moss) the functions of pots , soil , warmth and even watering can be combined <purpose> to make your planning and planting easier </purpose> </illustration> </instruction> .

<instruction> For best results , <verb type = action > set </verb> the plants in the garden on a cloudy morning <purpose> to help plants acclimate to the new soil </purpose> </instruction> .

<instruction> <verb type = action > Turn </verb> periodically with a garden fork <purpose> to allow air to circulate and feed organisms </purpose> , and decompose the organic matter quickly </instruction> .

Various examples from the do-it-yourself domain:

<instruction> Now , <verb type = action > go </verb> round opening the air bleed valves on the upstairs radiators <purpose> to allow air in to replace the water </purpose> </instruction> .

<instruction> <verb type = action > Close </verb> the drain cock and all the air bleed valves which were opened <purpose> to help drain the system </purpose> </instruction> .

<advice> <advice-concl> Choose waterproof paints as this is for a bathroom </advice-concl> </advice> .

<instruction> <condition> If you need to attach runners together due to the size of the room </condition> , <verb type = action> connect </verb> the ends where the slots and tabs are located and secure this connection with wire </instruction> .

<instruction> <circumstance> Once the armoire is primed </circumstance> , you <verb type = action > want </verb> <purpose> to start painting right away </purpose> </instruction> .

<instruction> The whole layer won't be visible <circumstance> once you start sponging </circumstance> , but you <verb type = action > want </verb> <purpose> to create the best base possible </purpose> </instruction> .

<warning> <warning-supp> To ensure that your existing door isn't weakened by your new lock , it should </ warning-supp > <warning-concl> not be more than three quarters of the overall thickness of the door </ warning-concl></warning> .

<warning> <warning-concl> Do not leave bagged - up paper indoors </ warning-concl><warning-supp > as it generates heat when compacted producing a possible fire hazard </ warning-supp > </warning> .

Conclusion

In this chapter, we have presented a description of the structure of a technical document, in particular the structure of a procedure. We have shown that, besides the backbone of a procedure, composed of titles and subtitles and instructions that realize the goals stated in titles, there is a whole set of linguistic structures that form what we call the explanation structure of a procedure. The explanation structure parallels the title-instruction structure. It is designed to guide the user of the procedure.

The explanation structure is in general quite simple: it is designed to help the user by making sure he understands the instructions and that he can evaluate his work. For that purpose we have developed a typology of E-functions and, via corpus analysis, a set of explanation schemes. We feel these structures can be considered as guidelines for technical writers.

This chapter ends by the description of the main structures of explanation functions as found in procedures. The structure of these functions turn out to be relatively simple and based on a limited set of linguistic marks, essentially discourse connectors. As a result, the description can be used in a number of domains.

In Chapter 5, we show how these structures can be implemented in Dislog and how they run in <TextCoop>. In Chapter 6, we investigate the structure of requirements, in particular security requirements, which is a specific class of technical documents. Requirements contain the same type of explanation functions than procedures, but with relatively different goals.

CHAPTER THREE

THE ART OF WRITING TECHNICAL DOCUMENTS

CAMILLE ALBERT, MATHILDE JANIER AND PATRICK SAINT-DIZIER

Introduction and Motivations

Most technical documents are produced by either engineers or by specialized technical writers. These documents are rarely produced from scratch: they are most of the time produced from already existing documents. Technical documents are indeed often the adaptation, the integration, the update or the revision of portions of previously existing documents. Technical writers often have a clear analysis of the limits and the risks of this authoring mode. In particular, the quality of writing may be less accurate and less homogeneous, with a lower cohesion. Missing paragraphs or pictures and inadequate references are frequent. Equipment uses and descriptions may not be totally updated. Finally, copy-paste operations may not be well controlled and authoring recommendations may not be fully followed.

The task of the technical writer is therefore quite complex and requires a lot of skills and care. In spite of a careful proofreading and possibly several validation steps, there always remain here and there errors which have more or less strong consequences on the task to carry out or on the use of the equipment which is being described. Technicians or operators using these documents must then manage these deficiencies via alternative solutions that they must elaborate themselves, in general with little help.

In most companies, technical writers must follow terminology, typographic and stylistic guidelines. This includes the appropriate use of terms (technical terms or business terms as well as general language terms), the structure of sentences, which must be rather simple, and the overall organization and style of the document. The objective is to make sure that technical documents are appropriate for operators, i.e., that they are understood, accepted, feasible and without any useless element.

In this chapter, we present a set of recommendations which are a synthesis of what is usually found in manuals dedicated to technical writing and in recommendations which are more specific to precise companies. Although the text is written in English and deals with recommendations for English, observations are very close or comparable for other languages. We have in particular elaborated a similar synthesis for the French language.

With respect to already existing literature, this chapter synthesizes elements found in (Weiss 1990, 1991), (Wright 2001), (O'Brian 2003), (Wyner et al. 2010) and (Alred et al. 2012). We also integrated recommendations coming from the *Simplified English* literature produced for the aeronautical domain. Besides references to manuals, useful Web sources are given in the bibliography section of this book. More specialized recommendations have also been integrated. These come from several companies working in different industrial areas: energy, transportation, chemistry, space, telecommunications, electronics and financial software. It is clear that each domain has different norms and a slightly different tradition. The target reader has also a major importance: engineers will react differently than inexperienced workers. Finally, we have observed and discussed with technical writers at work (Barcellini et al 2012) in seven companies, working in French or English, to have a better grasp at the importance of each type of recommendation.

In this chapter, we consider the various types of technical documents defined in Chapter 1: procedures, requirements and equipment or product manuals. It is important to note that we only consider in this book the written part of technical documents. Images, pictures and diagrams do play a major role in technical documentation production, but their analysis and impact on a task is a different problem. The same remark holds for the use of digital equipment such as tablets which is becoming increasingly important and will strongly influence technical document authoring and use.

The recommendations given below have been implemented in the LELIE system, within the framework of safety analysis and prevention. This system is briefly described in the last chapter of this book, Chapter 7.

General Quality Recommendations

To evaluate the quality of a technical document, the following criteria are advocated by (Alred et al. 2012), (Weiss 1990) and by most of the technical writing staff we have met. Those criteria remain relatively fuzzy and need to be made more precise and evaluated depending on the context of use: who is using it, with what frequency and in what situation. For example, the needs are different in emergency situations, or when users have the possibility to easily get help. These criteria are essentially simplicity, conciseness, cohesion (coherence is another type of problem related to the contents of the document), suitability, and clarity. These criteria motivate and organize the different authoring recommendations given in the next sections. They can roughly be characterized as follows:

Simplicity of expressions: (Alred et al. 2012) advise to use simple and direct terms, in particular verbs, especially for novice readers. These authors advise to use the following verbs: *try, press, stop, use, count, do, watch, divide*, while the "poor verb choice" must be avoided, e.g.: *attempt, depress, hit, discontinue, employ, enumerate, execute, observe, and segregate*. The same remark holds for other frequently used words such as manner adverbs and temporal expressions.

Conciseness of expressions and sentences: words, phrases, or even clauses must be removed when they turn out to be useless, but without sacrificing clarity or appropriate detail level. Note that conciseness is not a synonym for brevity: a long report may be very detailed, while its abstract may be brief and concise.

Cohesion of the document: the major components of a document must be written in a similar way, with a very stable use of terms and constructions. The terms (in particular acronyms, references and designations) must be used consistently, with a single term per object. Similarly, the typography, the symbols, the units and the acronyms must be used consistently and must remain unchanged throughout the whole document to facilitate its reading. Finally, the size of the sections of a document must also be balanced depending on their relative importance.

Suitability: analyses which documents are needed and aligns particular publications, manuals, examples and pictures with the tasks and interests of particular readers

Clarity and accuracy of sentences and titles: a precise word choice contributes to eliminate ambiguity and awkwardness. Similarly, a proper emphasis (i.e. stressing the most important ideas) and an adapted subordination are also crucial for achieving clarity. A clear text must be understood on the first reading.

A number of additional criteria are proper to requirements, they address their form as well as their contents in an accurate way. We consider in this book a variety of types of requirements from software to security requirements (this is developed in Chapter 6). These are summarized in the following chart (from Buddenberg 2012, personal communication):

Accuracy	Systems of requirements (SRS) must precisely define the system capabilities in a real-world environment, as well as how it interfaces and interacts with it. This aspect of requirements is a significant problem area for many SRSs.
Complete-ness	No necessary information should be missing. The requirements should be hierarchically organized in the requirement document to help reviewers understand the structure of the functionality described, so that it is easier for them to tell if something is missing.
Consis-tency	A requirement must not conflict or overlap with other requirements. A consistent document format must be used for writing requirements. Each specification document should use the same headings, fonts, indentions, and so forth. Templates can help: they act as checklists.
Correct-ness	The reference for correctness is the source of the requirement, such as an actual customer or a higher-level system requirement specification. Only user representatives can determine the correctness of user requirements. This is why it is essential to include them, or their close surrogates, to inspect the requirements.
Feasibility	It must be possible to implement or to realize each requirement within the known capabilities and limitations of the system and its environment.
Necessity or relevance	Each requirement should document something the customers really need or something that is required for conformance to an external requirement, an external interface, or a standard.
Revision	The requirement document must be revised when necessary and a history of the changes made on each requirement must be maintained. This is a part of traceability.
Objectivity	It is important to avoid value judgments via adjectives such as *easy, clear, effective, acceptable, suitable, good, bad, sufficient, useful*; also avoid subjective modals such as: *if possible, if necessary*

Prioritized	An implementation or usage priority must be assigned to each requirement, feature, or use case to indicate how essential it is to include it in a particular product release. Priority is a function of the value provided to the customer, the relative cost of implementation, and the relative technical risk associated with implementation or usage.
Tracea-bility	Each software requirement should be linked to its sources, which could be a higher-level system requirement, a use case, or voice-of-the-customer statements. Dates and authors should also be mentioned.
Non-ambiguous character	The reader of a requirement statement should be able to draw only one interpretation of it. Multiple readers of a requirement should reach the same interpretation.
Validity	Each requirement should be understood, analyzed, accepted, and approved by all parties and project participants. This is one of the main reasons SRSs are written using natural language.
Verifia-bility	Tests or other verification approaches, such as inspection or demonstration, should be used to determine whether each requirement is properly implemented in the product.

In the next sections of this chapter, we review in more depth a number of guidelines and recommendations for procedure and requirement authoring, based on the main criteria given above. Linguistic aspects include: lexical recommendations, business term choice, grammar and style recommendations. Finally, ergonomic recommendations are presented since they play an important role in connection with the linguistic aspects.

Lexical Recommendations

Lexical recommendations define the words or expressions to prefer when writing procedural documents. We survey here the main recommendations given in the literature or suggested by technical writers.

Buzz Words, Vague Terms

Buzzwords are words or phrases that suddenly become popular for non-rational reasons. Their meaning and usage tend to evolve rapidly and is, in general, relatively fuzzy. For these reasons they must be avoided. An interesting example is the case of *sophisticated* that now means exactly the reverse of its etymological sense.

Nouns such as *impact* and *interface* are buzzwords when they are used as verbs: they are fashionable but their meaning is too large to be used in technical documents.

The domain of finance is particularly rich in buzzwords: *A Ton of Money, Alternative Investment, Anatolian Tigers, Angelina Jolie Stock Index Anti-Fragility, Asian Century, At a Premium, Aunt Millie, Away From the Market, Baby Bells, Baby Boomer, etc.* These are difficult to precisely define for non-specialists and may also evolve (in particular their underlying positive or negative connotations).

As underlined by Weiss, some writers, in order to mimic an elaborated way of writing, use long words, where short, familiar words would have been just as effective. This must also be avoided whenever relevant, but not at the cost of precision: complex terms may convey nuances or may be more precise than shorter one. There is also in English the alternative choice of using a Germanic origin or Latin origin term (*cancel* vs. *delete*) which must be stabilized. These considerations can be briefly illustrated by the following table:

Replace	Possibly by
capability	ability
commencement	beginning
compensation, remuneration	pay
determination	choice
finalization	end
location	site, place
methodology	method
prioritization	ranking
requirement	need, wish
reservation	doubt
utilization	use
endeavour, essay, attempt	try
finalize, terminate	end
formulate, fabricate, construct	make
indicate, reveal, present, suggest	show, tell, say
initiate, commence	begin
inspect, ascertain, investigate	check
modify, alter, redesign	change

Jargon Terms

Jargon is a specialized slang language that is understandable only by a specific or a professional group. Jargon and complex legal wording must be replaced with familiar, concise words when possible.

Vague or fuzzy words are often common words that refer to general ideas, principles, materials and equipment, and, in a more abstract register, qualities, conditions, acts, or relationships. They should also be avoided when possible, more precise terms should be used instead.

Buddenberg suggests an interesting categorization of fuzzy terms to avoid in procedure instructions and in requirements:

Fuzzy terms to avoid	**Examples**
-*"below", "above"*	Instead of these terms, the structure "see + object", "following/preceding + object" should be preferred because it is more precise.
Vague adverbs	*very, quite, highly*
Vague adjectives	**Expressions of judgement**: *hard, slow, fast, hot, cold, low, high, easy, normal, adequate, effective, clear, acceptable, suitable, sufficient, useful* **Expressions of generality**: *large, rapid, many, timely, most, or close* **Evaluative words**: *real, nice, important, good, bad, contact, thing, fine.* **Order adjectives**: *First, then, next* **Vague location**: *Near, far, etc.* **Vague time**: *New, old, future, past, forthcoming*
Vague prepositions	*Above, in front, behind, near*
Vague verbs	**Inaccurate verbs**: *Increase, decrease* **Multi-use verbs**: *Do, be*
Verbs too generic	*Calculate, accept, verify, provide*, etc.
Undefined pronouns	*One, they, it* etc.
Demonstrative pronouns	*This one, these*, etc.
Subjective expressions	*may, if required, as appropriate*, or *if practical, if possible, if necessary.*

Weak Words, Phrases and Expressions

Weak phrases cause uncertainty and leave room for multiple interpretations and questions. They are a source of errors and risks in procedures or equipment manuals. Weak terms must be avoided. They include phrases such as: *as applicable, as appropriate, be able to, be capable of, but not limited to, tbd (to be continued).* In terms of connectors, *and* is probably the most ambiguous one, it includes temporal, causal and illustrative interpretations. It is better to avoid it when it is not used as a coordination.

Biased Language

Biased language refers to words and expressions that may offend because they make inappropriate assumptions or stereotypes about gender, ethnicity, physical or mental disability, age, or sexual orientation. For example:

Instead of →	Use:
Chairman/chairwoman	*chair, chairperson*
Foreman	*supervisor, manager*
Man-hours	*staff hours, worker hours*
Policeman, policewoman	*police officer*
Salesman, saleswoman	*salesperson*

Periphrases and Expression Length

Periphrases are long expressions, in terms of number of words that make sentences more complex to understand. These must be avoided and must be replaced by simple words.

Examples:

Replace: →	by:
Should it prove to be the case that	*if*
By means of the utilization of	*with, via*
At that earlier point in time	*then*
Make a distinction	*distinguish*
Accomplish linkage between	*link*
Have knowledge of	*know*
Reach a decision	*decide*
Form a plan	*plan*

Among these expressions, we can observe a number of light verb constructions composed of a generic verb such as *make* followed by a noun. In most cases, this construction can be replaced by the verb corresponding to the noun. In general, verbs must be preferred to nouns combined with light verbs because their form and style is more concise and direct.

The same situation is observed for *surplus* nouns, defined by (E. H. Weiss 1990 and 1991) as nouns that appear in phrases without adding any meaning or precision, such as *approach, problem, situation* or *type*. However, there are cases where these terms (including in this book) convey a general meaning which is appropriate: in this case, these must be kept to preserve the degree of generality of the presentation or of the description.

Excessive qualifications should also be avoided, especially in instructions. They may be used in warnings or requirements as a form of insistence. However, expressions such as *absolutely clear, totally committed* or *absolutely avoided* could be simplified and rephrased as: *clear, committed* or *avoided.*

Similarly, expressions that include forms of repetition should be avoided in most standard situations because they are mostly unproductive: *repeat again, visible to the eye, mixed together, complete stop*, etc.

There are several verbs which are not light verbs strictly speaking, but which have a low semantic impact in expressions or sentences, that should also be avoided. Verbs such as *serve* (*serves to justify*), *conduct (conduct a research*), *can* (*can rotate*), or *perform* or *carry out* (*perform an investigation*) fall in this class. It is not always easy to suppress these verbs, keeping and transforming the noun that follows into a verb. This should be considered whenever readability can be improved without altering understanding.

So far, we have shown that a number of expressions can be simplified by directly using the right term instead of compound constructions which add little if not no meaning. There are also symmetric situations where it is preferable to keep all the words in a sentence. In particular, prepositions and articles such as *the* or *a*, should not be suppressed. Without them, sentences are composed of sequences of nouns and verbs that are difficult to understand.

Authors such as Weiss suggest to avoid using the third person in instructions. Consider for example:

The operator then enters his or her security status.

A more neutral formulation should be preferred, unless there are several actors in the procedure (which may happen in complex procedures):

Enter your security status.

Similarly, adverbs must be placed where they are operational so that their scope is clearly identified:

Only write corrections, not changes, on the worksheet vs.
Write corrections, not changes, only on the worksheet.

Technical or Business Terms versus Standard Terms

A number of companies require the use of very precise technical terms from their domain ontology or terminology instead of large public or imprecise terms. These concern essentially nouns that designate equipment, products, locations, etc. This is an important issue that requires an analysis of the terms to be used in procedures or in requirements. An important issue is then the maintenance of procedures and requirements when the terminology evolves or when an equipment becomes obsolete and is replaced by another one. Complex revisions are necessary that may lead to additional errors.

The same situation is often observed for the verbs which are used. In large public applications, the number and diversity of verbs found in procedures is often very large. Some may be largely metaphorical and difficult to interpret. For example, the cooking domain counts about 300 frequently used verbs whereas the Do-It-Yourself and Gardening domains count more than 700 verbs. This very high number of verbs is in general not accepted in professional documents where the number of verbs is often limited to about 100. Limiting the number of verbs to those which are necessary is also an important recommendation when producing technical documents.

In Summary

In order to improve the quality of a technical document, in normal conditions, we advise to:

- use the simplest words appropriate to the intent of the statement,
- use the shortest expressions: these are in general sufficiently clear and explicit,
- use the proper expression or sentence structures,
- select words and phrases based on their formal definitions, not what the popular culture thinks they mean,
- write simple and direct statements.

Syntactic and Stylistic Recommendations

Syntactic and stylistic recommendations define the way words, phrases, and clauses combine together to form unambiguous and easily understandable sentences. Let us briefly review in this section a number of recommendations given in the literature or usually practiced by technical writers.

Dealing with References

It is first essential to care about the use of pronominal or temporal references. If pronouns are necessary to produce short and fluid sentences, their antecedents must be easy to identify. For example, it is suggested to replace *it* used as a subject or an object by its referent, even if this introduces a repetition. The impersonal use of *it* must remain unchanged (*it is possible…*). It is also advised not to use *this* as a clausal subject or object, and, in general, to avoid demonstrative pronouns (*this one, these*, etc.), and undefined pronouns (*one, they*, etc.). The same remark holds for sentences starting with *there is, there are*. New paragraphs should never start by a pronoun.

Sentence Structure and Organization

It is often recommended, in order to limit the reader's effort, to use parallel structures in elements such as enumerations, repetitive (or very similar) sequences of instructions and chart cells. This means that sentence elements that fulfil a given function in instructions, enumerations or chart cells must have a similar grammatical form. Parallel structures reduce intellectual effort; they clarify meaning, improve the quality of the text, and facilitate instruction execution. Parallel structures are convenient for readers because they allow them to anticipate the role of a sentence on the basis of its construction. Parallel structures can be achieved with words, phrases, or clauses. However, there is a risk of a monotonous discourse that must be avoided; therefore, slight term variations can be used, as in the following set of requirements:

The provider has to mention in the roadmap the support for the different network protocols …

The provider has to mention the support of VL, Q to Q …

The provider must mention the support of high bandwidth probes which are addressing IP7 high bandwidth …

The provider shall detail the roadmap for the support of IP V9 whatever the level: User Plane …

The provider shall explain how the hardware…

In this short example, modals such as *must, shall* and *has to* are used to avoid a very monotonous discourse. Their strength is relatively similar, there is therefore no priority implicitly introduced between these four requirements. In general, it is recommended that in a sequence of enumerative elements, all the elements share the same structure for the three to five first words.

In terms of length, it is crucial to avoid long sentences. Length depends on the domain, the situation (emergency or repetitive operation) and also on the reading capacity of the user. Recommendations vary in general between a maximum of 15 to 40 words. This interval is quite large: it reflects the diversity of instructions and the potential complexity of actions to carry out. Complexity may also come from the terms which are used: long sentences with standard language are easier to understand than shorter ones which essentially contain technical terms. Complex instructions must be short when possible, or decomposed into several shorter ones. Similarly, long paragraphs (more than one page) must be avoided because it is difficult to keep in mind the main ideas they convey.

Basic sentence form is the subject-verb-object-(indirect object) pattern, which is familiar to readers. Simple sentences are essential to guarantee an easy comprehension of instructions. Furthermore, such a construction guarantees a form of completion: a visual inspection is sufficient to make sure that the object and possibly the oblique or indirect object are realized. This is crucial when e.g. equipment or values must be given to correctly perform an instruction.

Word order is an important issue. When the subject is not required, the main verb is often expected first, followed by its complements. However, when conditions or purposes are very critical, they may appear first in order to put emphasis on them. Authors such as (Alred, 2012), in order to make sentences more interesting, suggest to:

- start with a modifying word, phrase, or clause,
- invert word order, which is an effective way to achieve variety,
- alter normal sentence order by inserting a phrase or a clause (for achieving emphasis, providing detail, breaking monotony, and regulating pace).

This view may be of interest when producing large public procedures (e.g. gardening) but it seems that this practice is not frequently encountered or even recommended in companies' guidelines.

Finally, the active voice must be privileged over the passive voice since the latter tends to evade responsibility and to obscure issues, thus leading to unclear instructions.

At a more global level, when describing a process, the use of transitional words and phrases creates unity within paragraphs. A good specification of headings also provides transition from one step to another.

It is difficult to give recommendations for style since it heavily depends on the domain and the type of document being produced. General style recommendations are often given in companies' recommendations. For example, formulate applicability conditions, then instructions and then the purpose of the task.

Syntactic Structures to Avoid

Assertive sentences are less ambiguous than negative constructions. It is recommended to use a maximum of one negation marker per sentence when there is no possibility to use a construction without a negation. Double negation must be avoided.

Modals such as *should, could*, etc., which are used for the conditional mode, must be avoided in instructions. The auxiliaries *must* and *shall* can be used in the present tense for greater consistency and precision in instructions, to mark their importance. However, these auxiliaries are more commonly typical of requirements and warnings.

Constructions in the passive voice or in the future must be avoided in particular in instructions and in requirements.

Strings of words in English, e.g. sequences of nouns, must be avoided because they may be ambiguous and therefore may require some understanding effort. Even a two-word string like *management option* could mean:

-an option available to management,

-one of several ways to manage,

-the choice of having management or not.

Strings of nouns are tolerable when they are names of systems, or parts of systems (*local area network conversion protocol*), or well-known technical terms of a domain or when they are fully explained the first time they are introduced. In other contexts, though, they are cryptic and, therefore, must be avoided. For example:

graphics construction language should be reformulated as :

language for constructing graphics.

Similarly: *operator-induced failure problem*

must be reformulated as:

a problem of failure induced by the operator.

The same problem occurs with stacks of modifiers. These modifiers are often adjectives and adverbs. When two or more modifiers appear before a noun, the meaning of the phrase is usually clear only to the writer. Be especially careful of cases in which the first modifier could modify either the second modifier or the noun.

The technical writers we have met and observed have also indicated that embedded relative clauses or even sequences of relative clauses in an instruction must be avoided. In general, a single relative clause in an instruction should be sufficient. Similarly, long sequences of coordinated elements, using either *and* or *or*, or *either... or*, or combinations of them, must be avoided when possible. It is obviously not recommended to have a coordination with a combination of *and* and *or*. Finally, and for the same reasons, long sequences of noun complements must be avoided.

To conclude this section, and as a matter of exemplification of the principles we have stated, let us present a few figures that give a general estimate of the importance of the recommendations given in the previous sections. The following chart relates an analysis we carried out within the framework of our LELIE project (Chapter 7) to characterize the frequency of the main errors found in technical documents. The figures given below (Table 3-1) have been realized on a variety of documents in French from three companies in different sectors (energy, transportation and chemistry). Figures given in this chart are given for 1000 lines of text:

Type of error	**Error severity level**	**Average frequency per 1000 lines**
Fuzzy terms	high	66
Use of modals	medium	21
Light verb constructions	medium	15
Personal pronouns	medium to high	27
Complex pronoun resolution	high	33
Negation in instructions	high	52
Too many subordinate clauses	high	7
Too many conjunctions	medium	17
Incorrect position of specific terms (e.g. verbs)	medium	56
Too many noun complements	medium to high	36
Use of passive constructions	medium	34
Sentence length	high	108
Irregularities in enumerations	high	43
Incorrect cross references	high	33

Table 3-1 Error rates in technical documents

These results show that errors in technical documents are very frequent, in spite of recommendations. Therefore, either several levels of validations and proofreading are necessary or a system such as LELIE must be used.

This chart is simply indicative of the different types of errors made by technical writers and of their relative frequency. There are major differences between companies and the type of document considered. It is important to note that sometimes errors cannot be avoided, and in fact should not be considered as errors. For example, in the case of negation it may be very difficult to find a positive counterpart, as in:

Do not throw in the sewer.

Then, if the right recipient is not known (e.g. a type of garbage can) it may be difficult to avoid the negation. Such a statement is of interest since it puts emphasis on the sewer that must not be used. Similarly, there are categories of terms which are fuzzier than others, possibly in some specific contexts, and depending on the domain some of them may be accepted. This is for example the case of manner adverbs (*progressively, cautiously*), as in:

progressively close the valve,

since it is a relatively short action. In general, fuzzy quantifiers are not accepted (*press for a few seconds*). In this latter case, it is preferable to give e.g. an interval, *between 5 and 9 seconds.*

In the above chart, sentence length is declared inappropriate above 40 words including determiners and prepositions. "Incorrect cross-references" refers to references which are not appropriate, for example, *see 4.5* and that section does not exist or refers to something that is not relevant to the technical elements at stake.

Ergonomic Recommendations

The overall ergonomics of a document is also a major contribution to its quality, particularly its ability to help users to better understand procedures. It is important to keep in mind that procedural documents may be very large, beyond 100 pages, therefore an adequate and well-designed layout is crucial.

First, the manual must be designed so that readers can use the equipment, software, tool or machinery while they are also reading the instructions.

In terms of its overall structure, the document must follow a number of principles. First, an ***overview*** at the beginning of a manual is important and useful; its role is to explain:

- the overall purpose of the procedure,

- how the procedure can be useful to the reader and
- any precautions or warnings the reader should know and keep in mind before starting.

If readers know the purpose of the procedure, they will be more likely to pay attention to the steps of the procedure and apply them appropriately in the future.

It is important to define terms that readers might not immediately understand in a ***glossary*** or data dictionary. This is in particular useful for large documents.

Headings and subheadings should be formulated with words that readers find familiar so that they can easily locate particular sections and instructions. They should be reasonably short, but explicit. It is recommended that they are not elliptic, i.e. that they contain at least a verb and its direct object. For example, *"the topping"* is not an appropriate title, but *"preparing the topping"* is much more acceptable. Verbs should be formulated in the infinitive form, (*to scan the document*) or in the gerund form (*scanning the document*). The same syntax should be used throughout the entire document. Headings should be quite frequent so that the reader has a good perception of the overall structure of the task.

Headings and subheadings are important to indicate the goals of instructions: they must be well structured, in a top down manner, with a reasonable level of decomposition. In general three levels of decomposition is sufficient. The title-subtitle hierarchy must be clear. For example, titles and subtitles must receive an appropriate and clear numbering or typography that reflects the title-subtitle hierarchy. For clarity purposes, complex procedures should be divided into separate tasks, and sections with appropriate titles should be defined to cover them. These tasks should also be described in the section headings and in the procedure introduction.

Instructions are easy to follow when they are divided into short, simple steps in their proper sequence (steps can be organized with words such as: *first, then, finally*, or with numbers). When appropriate, the expected result of an action should be indicated to confirm readers that they are performing the procedure correctly. For example:

A blinking light will appear.

You will see a red triangle.

Visuals (pictures, diagrams, charts, graphics, etc.) are useful elements in a procedure. They are not addressed in this book because they constitute a different problem. They contribute to illustrating ideas conveyed by words in instructions. They tend to have a stronger impact than words regarding some types of information such as the depiction of processes or relationships, the representation of numbers and quantities, drawings, photographs, maps, etc. Visuals must be clearly drawn and labelled to show readers exactly what equipment, online screens, or any other items they use should look like. However, they must be up to date in order not to add any confusion (e.g. an old equipment, different from the one being used, will puzzle the user).

Buddenberg, among others, stresses the importance of directives, which are categories of words and phrases that index or indicate illustrative information. They include words such as *Figure, Table, For example, Note.*

In several types of style sheets, company recommendations rely mostly on the coordination of visual and textual elements, aiming at clearer instructions, and therefore fewer errors on the part of the technicians. For example, a group of instructions in natural language is placed on odd pages, while complementary information, charts, diagrams or pictures are located on the opposite page.

Similarly, readers are alerted of any potentially hazardous materials before they reach the step for which the material is needed. This is realized via appropriate logos or icons, always given at the same place in the document, e.g. at the top or in the margin of the left-hand page.

Each ***reference*** cited should be identified with a unique number or identifier. References should be cited by a short title, full title, version or release designator, date, publisher or source, and document number or any other unique document identifier. It is important to use a unique citation identifier when referencing information in the cited document.

Finally, to make sure that the reader understanding is correct, illustrations should be used as often as possible. Examples in instructions or in requirements must follow the following considerations:

-Illustration and Example: what is to be illustrated should be immediately followed with the example.

-Repetition of an example: An example can be repeated if it is not already located on the same page. It is better to be repetitive than to divert the reader's attention.

-Verification of the validity of the example: it is important to ensure that the example is valid and explicit.

Controlled Languages

Most of the restrictions given above for producing technical documents in general are also found in controlled language recommendations. In fact, goals are quite similar. Let us briefly advocate them here.

Controlled Language (CL) is a form of language with specific restrictions on grammar, style, and vocabulary usage, designed to allow domain specialists to unambiguously formulate texts pertaining to their subject fields. CLs apply to specialized sublanguages of particular domains, and to technical documents, including instructions, procedures, descriptions, reports, and requirements. Documents are often structured in XML and stored in dedicated textual databases. This has an impact on the way these documents are written and updated.

Controlled Language originates from the Caterpillar Fundamental English (CFE) introduced in the 1960s. It then evolved to form the basis for the simplified English used by the Carnegie-Mellon KANT project involving machine translation of the Caterpillar Tractor Company's maintenance manuals for heavy equipment exported worldwide.

One of the most popular recent controlled language is the AECMA Simplified English, adopted by an entire industry, the aerospace industry, and developed to facilitate the use of maintenance manuals by non-native speakers of English. Controlled language facilitates human-human communication (e.g. translation or technical documentation) and human-machine communication (e.g. interfaces with databases or automated inference engines). A number of features on this topic are developed in (O'Brien, 2003). See also a large number of Web sources cited in the reference section of this book.

According to (Wyner 2010), more than 40 CNLs have been introduced up to now, covering languages such as English, Esperanto, French, German, Greek, Japanese, Mandarin, Spanish, and Swedish. Two main types of CNLs can be identified:

- Human-Oriented Controlled Language (HOCL): which is the basis for the AECMA SE
- Machine-Oriented Controlled Language (MOCL): used for example at Boeing and IBM.

In her article *Controlling Controlled English. An Analysis of Several Controlled Language Rule Sets,* Sharon O'Brien, relies on the concept of *primary functionality* in order to classify CL rules. Three categories are defined roughly as follows:

- ***Lexical***: if the primary function of the rule is to influence word selection or to influence meaning by word selection, then it is classified as a lexical rule. This is a major component since most CL environments are related to the domain ontology and terminology. Besides the terminology, some terms are preferred to others, for example because of their greater accuracy in the company's domain.
- ***Syntactic***: if the primary function of the rule is to influence syntax, then the rule is classified as a syntactic rule.

- ***Textual***: the “textual” category is sub-divided into “text structure” and “pragmatic” rules, depending on the primary function of the rule:
  - -If the primary function of the rule is to influence the graphic layout or information load in the text, then it is classified as a text structure rule.
  - -If the primary function of the rule is to influence text purpose or reader response to the text, then it is classified as a pragmatic rule.

To end this section on controlled languages, let us note the norm SBVR, standing for Semantics of Business Vocabulary and Business Rules, which is an OMG specification. SBVR introduces very strict constraints on vocabulary and structure for the description of business rules dedicated to the definition of products. This norm is still under testing in a small number of companies, it is however a very promising approach for technical documents.

Conclusion

In this chapter, we have presented a synthesis of recommendations and guidelines for writing technical documents. These recommendations concern business terms as well as the lexical, syntactic, semantic and stylistic levels of any technical document. We have also included a few ergonomic considerations and elements related to controlled language recommendations which are very close to the considerations on authoring documents we have focused on. The elements presented in this chapter are a synthesis of a number of books and manuals on technical document authoring, authoring recommendations proper to various companies, with their own views and evaluations on technical documentation and, finally, discussions we had with technical writers at work. An important feature is that what is identified as an "error" in technical writing may be perfectly acceptable in ordinary language.

There are obviously major differences in the evaluation of the severity of an error depending on the company, its target readers (e.g. beginners vs. confirmed technicians or engineers), and its know-how and traditions. There are also major differences in what should be avoided and the ways to resolve writing difficulties. In Chapter 7 of this book, we present the Lelie project where, precisely, the type of error to detect and it severity level can be parameterized so that a system can be customized to a certain authoring activity in a given company. The severity of an error can also be contextualized so that only those which are really crucial to the understanding of a document can be outlined. Correcting an error may indeed be very costly, e.g. correcting a fuzzy term may need to consult a lot of documents.

There are a few tools, more or less recent, available on the market that implement some principles of controlled language recommendations. Let us note *Acrocheck, Hunt overrides* and *Madpack*. There are a few systems based on the notion of boilerplates (see Chapter 6) such as RAT-RQA developed by the *reusecompany*. A number of companies have their own recommendations and related internal system with specific properties and functions, these are not distributed on the market.

CHAPTER FOUR

AN INTRODUCTION TO TEXTCOOP AND DISLOG

PATRICK SAINT-DIZIER

Introduction

In this chapter, we first introduce the foundational elements which are at the basis of the programming language Dislog and the platform <TextCoop> on which Dislog runs. Dislog has been primarily designed for discourse processing; it can in particular recognize the structures presented in Chapter 2. It can also be used in other contexts where the recognition of complex patterns in texts is a central issue. In Chapter 7, dedicated to the Lelie project, we show how Dislog can be used to help technical writers to improve the quality of their documents. Dislog is based on logic and logic programming and offers a declarative way of describing linguistic structures. It integrates reasoning components and offers a very modular way of describing language phenomena.

The Dislog language (Dislog stands for *Discourse in logic*, or discontinuities in logic since discourse structure analysis is based on marks which often are in long-distance dependency relations) is presented in detail in this chapter. The <TextCoop> platform is then introduced, in particular the <TextCoop> engine and the linguistic architecture of the system. Dislog is illustrated in the chapters that follow. Finally, we present and discuss in this chapter performance issues which are crucial since processing the discourse structure of texts is in general not very efficient due to the size of texts, which are often large, and the complexity and ambiguity of discourse structures. The <TextCoop> platform is freely available from the author.

There are at the moment a few well-known and widely used language processing environments. They are essentially used for sentence processing, not for discourse analysis. The reasons are essentially that sentences and their substructures are the main level of analysis for a large number of applications such as information extraction, opinion analysis based on the structure evaluative expressions, or machine translation. Discourse analysis turns out to be not so critical for these applications. However, applications such as automatic summarization (Marcu 2000) or question-answering do require an intensive discourse analysis level, as shown in (Jin et al. 1987).

Dedicated to sentence processing, let us note the GATE platform (http://gate.ac.uk/) which is widely used, and the Linguastream (http://www.linguastream.org) system which is based on a component architecture, making this system really flexible. Besides some specific features to deal with simple aspects of discourse processing, none of these platforms allow the specification of rules for an extensive discourse analysis nor the introduction of reasoning aspects, which is however essential to introduce pragmatic considerations into discourse processing. GATE is used e.g. for semantic annotation, corpus construction, knowledge acquisition and information extraction, summarization, and investigations around the semantic web. It also includes research on audio, vision and language connections. Linguastream has components that mainly deal with part of speech and syntactic analysis. It also handles several types of semantic data with a convenient modular approach. It is widely used for corpus analysis. In a different context, the GETARUNS system (http://project.cgm.unive.it/getaruns.html), based on the LFG grammar approach, has some capabilities to process simple forms of discourse structures and can realize some forms of argumentation analysis. Finally, (Marcu 2000) developed a discourse analyzer for the purpose of automatic summarization. This system is based on the RST assumptions, which are not always realistic in a number of contexts, as developed in the section below.

Within a very different perspective, and inspired by sentence syntax, two approaches based on Tree Adjoining Grammars (TAGs) (Gardent 1997) and (Webber et al. 2004), extend the formalism of TAGs to the processing of discourse structures via tree anchoring mechanisms. The approach remains essentially lexically based. It is aimed at connecting propositions related by various discourse connectors or at relating text spans which are in a referential relation.

Some Linguistic Considerations

Most works dedicated to discourse analysis have to deal with the triad: discourse structure identification, delimitation of its textual structure (boundaries of the discourse unit, sometimes called elementary discourse unit or EDU) and discourse structure binding to form larger structures representing the articulations of a whole text. By structure identification, we mean identifying a kernel or a satellite of e.g. a rhetorical relation, such as an illustration, an illustrated expression, an elaboration, or the elaborated expression, a conditional expression, a goal expression, etc. as those presented in Chapter 2. Discourse structures are realized by textual structures which need to be accurately delimited. These are then not isolated: they must be bound to other structures, based on the kernel-satellite or kernel-kernel principle, introduced in Chapter 2.

<TextCoop> and Dislog are based on the following features and constraints:

- ***discourse structure identification***: identifying a basic discourse structure (e.g. the EES defined in Chapter 2) requires a comprehensive specification of the lexical, syntactic, morphological, punctuation and possibly typographic marks (Luc et al 1999), (Longacre 1982) that allow the identification of this discourse function. In general the recognition of satellite functions is easier than the recognition of their corresponding kernel(s) because they are more strongly marked. For example, it is quite straightforward to recognize an illustration (although we had to define 20 generic rules that describe this structure), but identifying the exact text span which is its kernel (i.e. what is illustrated) is much more ambiguous. Similarly, the support of an argument is marked much more explicitly than its conclusion.
- ***structure or text span delimitation***: most of the literature on discourse analysis dedicated to the delimitation of discourse units refers either to Elementary Discourse Units (EDUs) (Schauer 2006), or to the vague notion of text span. When identifying discourse structures in texts, finding their textual boundaries is very challenging. In addition, contrary to the assumptions of RST (e.g. (Grosz et al. 1986), (Marcu 2000)) several partly overlapping textual units can be involved in different discourse relations.
- ***binding discourse units***: the last challenge is, given a set of discourse structures, to identify relations between them. For example, relating an illustration and the illustrated element, which are not necessarily adjacent. Similarly, argument conclusions and supports are difficult to relate. These may not necessarily be contiguous: independent discourse functions may be inserted between them. We also observed a number of one-to-many relations (e.g. various reformulations of a given element), besides the standard one-to-one relations. Similarly, an argument conclusion may have several

supports, possibly with different orientations. As a consequence, the principle of textual contiguity cannot be applied systematically. For that purpose, we have developed a principle called selective binding, which is also found in formal syntax to deal with long-distance dependencies or movement theory.

Some Foundational Principles of Dislog

In Chapter 2, a number of challenging discourse processing situations have been outlined. The necessity of a modular approach, where each aspect of discourse analysis and each type of function and constraint is dealt with accurately in a specific module, has lead us to consider some simple elements of the model of Generative Syntax (a good synthesis is given in (Lasnik et al. 1988)).

In the Dislog approach, we consider:

- ***productive principles***, which have a high level of abstraction, which are linguistically sound, but which may be too powerful,
- ***restrictive principles***, which limit the power of the productive principles on the basis of well-formedness constraints.

Another foundational feature is an integrated view of marks used to identify discourse functions, merging lexical elements with morphological functions, typography and punctuation, syntactic constructs, semantic features and inferential patterns that capture various forms of knowledge (domain, lexical, textual). <TextCoop> is the first platform that offers this view within a logic-based approach.

If machine learning is a possible approach for sentence processing, where interesting results have emerged, it seems not to be so successful for discourse analysis (e.g. (Carlson et al. 2001)). This is due to two main factors: (1) the difficulty to annotate discourse functions in texts (Saaba et al 2008) characterized by the high level of disagreement between annotators and (2) the large non-determinism encountered when processing discourse structures where linguistic marks are often immerged in long spans of text of no or little interest. For these reasons, we adopted a rule-based approach. Rules may be hand coded, based on corpus analysis using bootstrapping tools, or may emerge from a supervised learning method.

Dislog rules basically implement productive principles. Rules are composed of three main parts:

- ***a discourse function identification structure***, which basically has the form of a rule or a pattern,
- ***a set of calls to inferential forms*** using various types of knowledge. These forms are part of the identification structure, they may

contribute to solving ambiguities, they may also be involved in the computation of the resulting representation or they may express semantic or pragmatic restrictions. This is developed below on page 85,

- ***a structure that represents the result*** of the analysis: it can be the same text associated with simple XML structures, or any other structure such as a graph or a dependency structure. More complex representations, e.g. based on primitives, can be computed using a rich semantic lexicon. This is of much interest for an analysis oriented towards a conceptual analysis of discourse.

Besides rules, Dislog allows the specification of a number of ***restrictive principles***, expressed as active constraints, e.g. dominance, precedence, exclusion, etc. as shall be seen below. The restrictions introduced by these principles are checked throughout the whole parsing process.

The Structure of Dislog Rules

Let us now introduce in more depth the structure of Dislog rules. Dislog follows the principles of logic-based grammars as implemented three decades ago in a series of formalisms, among which, most notably: Metamorphosis Grammars (Colmerauer 1978), Definite Clause Grammars (Pereira and Warren 1980) and Extraposition Grammars (Pereira 1981). These formalisms were all designed for sentence parsing with an implementation in Prolog via a meta-interpreter or a direct translation into Prolog. Illustrations are given in (Saint-Dizier 1994). The last two formalisms include a simple device to deal with long distance dependencies. Various processing strategies have been investigated in particular bottom-up parsing, parallel parsing, constraint-based parsing and an implementation of the Earley algorithm that merges bottom-up analysis with top-down predictions. These systems have been used in applications, with reasonable efficiency and a real flexibility to updates, as reported in e.g. (Gazdar et al. 1989).

Dislog adapts and extends these grammar formalisms to discourse processing, it also extends the regular expression format which is often used as a basis in language processing tools. The rule system of Dislog is viewed as a set of productive principles representing the different language forms taken by discourse structures.

A rule in Dislog has the following general form, which is quite close to Definite Clause Grammars and Metamorphosis Grammars from a syntactic and semantic point of view:

L(Representation) --> R, {P}.

where:

- L is a non-terminal symbol.
- Representation is the representation resulting from the analysis, it is in general an XML structure with attributes that annotate the original text. It can also be a partial dependency structure or a more formal representation.
- R is a sequence of symbols as described below, and
- P is a set of predicates and functions implemented in Prolog that realize the various computations and controls, and that allow the inclusion of inference and knowledge into rules. These are included between curly brackets as in logic grammars to differentiate them from grammar symbols.

R is a finite sequence of the following elements:

- ***terminal symbols*** that represent words, expressions, punctuations, various existing html or XML tags. They are included between square brackets in the rules,
- ***preterminal symbols***: are symbols which are derived directly into terminal elements. These are used to capture various forms of generalizations, facilitating rule authoring and update. They should be preferred to terminal elements when generalizations over terminal elements are possible. Symbols can be associated with a type feature structure that encodes a variety of aspects from morphology to semantics,
- ***non-terminal symbols***, which can also be associated with type feature structures. These symbols refer to "local grammars", i.e. grammars that encode specific syntactic constructions such as temporal expressions or domain specific constructs. Non-terminal symbols do not include discourse structure symbols: Dislog rules cannot call each other, this feature is dealt with by the selective binding principle, which includes additional controls. A rule in Dislog encodes the recognition of a discourse function taken in isolation.
- ***optionality and iteration marks*** over non-terminal and preterminal symbols, as in regular expressions,
- ***gaps***, which are symbols that stand for a finite sequence of words of no present interest for the rule which must be skipped. A gap can appear only between terminal, preterminal or non-terminal symbols. Dislog offers the possibility to specify in a gap a list of elements which must not be skipped: when such an element is found before the termination of the gap, then the gap fails. The length of the skipped string can also be controlled. A ***skip*** predicate

is also included in the language: it is close to a gap and simply allows the system to skip a maximum number of words given as a parameter.
- ***a few meta-predicates*** to facilitate rule authoring.

Symbols in a rule may have any number of arguments. However, in our current version, to facilitate the implementation of the meta-interpreter and to improve its efficiency, the recommended form is:

identifier(Representation, Typed feature structure).

where Representation is the symbol's representation. In Prolog format, a difference list (E,S) is added at the end of the symbol:

identifier(R, TFS, E, S)

The typed feature structure (TFS) can be an ordered list of features, in Prolog style, or a list of attribute-value pairs. Examples are developed in the next chapter.

Similarly to DCGs and to Prolog clauses, it is possible and often necessary to have several rules to fully describe the different realizations of a given discourse function. They all have the same identifier Ident, as it is the case e.g. for the rules that describe NPs or PPs. A set of rules with the same identifier is called a ***cluster of rules***. Rule in a cluster are executed sequentially, in their reading order, from the first to the last one, by the <TextCoop> engine. Then, clusters are called in the order they are given in a ***cascade***. This is explained below.

As an illustration, let us consider a generic rule that describes conditional expressions, given in Chapter 2:

```
Condition(R) -->
conn(cond,_), gap(G), ponct(comma).
```

with:

```
conn(cond,_) --> if.
```

For example, in the following sentences, the underlined structures are identified as conditions:

If all of the sources seem to be written by the same person or group of people*, you must again seriously consider the validity of the topic.*

If you put too many different themes into one body paragraph*, then the essay becomes confusing.*

For essay conclusions, don't be afraid to be short and sweet ***if you feel that the argument's been well-made****.*

The gap G covers the entire conditional statement between the mark *if* and the comma. The argument R in the above rule contains a representation of the discourse structure, for example, in XML:

<condition> .... </condition>....

<condition> If all of the sources seem to be written by the same person or group of people, </condition> you must again seriously consider the validity of the topic.

There are obviously several rules to identify the different forms of conditional expressions, some of them are given in Chapter 2.

Dislog Advanced Features

In this section, we describe the features offered by the Dislog language that complement the grammar rule system. These mostly play the role of restrictive principles. At the moment we have defined three sets of devices: selective binding rules to link discourse units identified by the rule system, correction rules to revise incorrect representations e.g. erroneously placed tags made by previous rules, and concurrency statements that allow a correct management of clusters of rules. Concurrency statements are closely related to the cascade system. They are constrained by the notion of bounding node, which delimits the text portion in which discourse units can be bound. Similarities with sentence formal syntax are outlined when appropriate, however, phenomena at discourse level are substantially different.

Selective Binding Rules

Selective binding rules are the means offered by Dislog to construct hierarchical discourse structures from elementary ones (discourse functions), identified by the rule system. Selective binding rules allow the system to link two or more already identified discourse functions. The objective is e.g. to bind a kernel with a satellite (e.g. an argument conclusion with its support) or with another kernel (e.g. for the concession or parallel relations).

Related to this latter situation is the binding of two argument conclusions, which e.g. share a similar support, as in:

Do not use butter to cook vegetables because it contains too much cholesterol, similarly, avoid palm oil.

The *similarly* linguistic mark binds two argument conclusions related to the same topic. This mark introduces a kind of ellipsis. Selective binding rules can be used for other purposes than implementing rhetorical relations. These can be used more generally to bind any kind of structure in application domains. For example, in procedural discourse, they can be used to link a title with the set of instructions, prerequisites and warnings that realize the goal expressed by this title.

From a syntactic point of view, selective binding rules are expressed using the Dislog language formalism. Different situations occur that make binding rules more complex than any system of rules used for sentence processing, in particular:

- discourse structures may be embedded to a high degree, with partial overlaps,
- they may be chained (a satellite is a kernel for another relation),
- kernels and related satellites may be non-adjacent,
- kernels may be linked to several satellites of different types,
- some satellites may be embedded into their kernel.

Selective binding rules allow the binding of:

- two adjacent structures, in general a kernel and a satellite, or another kernel. A standard case is an argument conclusion followed by its support.
- more than two adjacent structures, a kernel and several satellites. For example, it is quite common to have an argument conclusion associated with several supports, possibly with different orientations: *The Maoists will win the elections because they have a large audience and because they threat Terrai tribe leaders.*
- two or more non-adjacent structures, which may be separated by various elements (e.g. causes and consequences, conclusion and supports may be separated by various elements). This is a frequent situation in everyday language, where previous items are referred to via pronominal references or via various kinds of marks (e.g. *coming back to*): *Avoid seeding by high winds. Avoid also frost periods. Besides the fact that the wind will disperse most of your seeds, your vegetables will not grow where you expect them to be.*

However limits must be imposed on the "textual distance" between units. In discourse, such a constraint is not related to well-formedness constraints as it is in sentence syntax, but it captures the fact that units which are very distant (e.g. several paragraphs) are very difficult to conceptually relate. One of the reasons is that focus or even topic shifts are frequent over paragraphs or sections and memorizing the topic chain is somewhat difficult.

In terms of representation, the two first cases above can be dealt with using a standard XML notation where the different structures are embedded into a parent XML structure that represents the whole structure.

This is realized via the use of logic variables in logic programming which offer a very powerful declarative approach to structure building. The latter case requires a different kind of representation technique. We adopt a notation similar to the neo-Davidsonian notation used for events in sentence logical representations (Davidson 1963). An ID, which can be interpreted as a discourse event, is associated with each tagged discourse function.

A selective binding rule for two adjacent structures can then be stated as follows:

```
argument(R) -->
   [<conclusion>], gap(G1), [</conclusion>],
    connector(C,[type:cause]), [<support>], gap(G2), [</support>].
```

where the first gap covers the conclusion (textual unit G1) and the second one covers the support (textual unit G2), the connector is defined by C, with the constraint that it is of type cause.

To limit the textual distance between argument units, we introduce the notion of ***bounding node***, which is also a notion used in sentence formal syntax to restrict the way long-distance dependencies can be established (Lasnik et al. 1988). Bounding nodes are also defined in terms of barriers in Generative syntax (Chomsky 1986). In our case, the constraint is that a gap must not go over a bounding node. This allows the system to restrict the distance between the constituents which are bound.

For example, we consider that an elaboration and the elaborated element or an argument conclusion and its support must be in the same paragraph, therefore, the node "paragraph" is a bounding node. This declaration is taken into account by the <TextCoop> engine in a transparent way, and interpreted as an active constraint which must be valid throughout the whole parsing process.

The situation is however more complex than in sentence syntax. Indeed, bounding nodes in discourse depend on the structure being processed. For example, in the case of procedural discourse, a warning can be bound in general to one or more instructions which are in the same sub-goal structure. Therefore, the bounding node will be the sub-goal node, which may be much larger than a paragraph.

Bounding nodes are declared as follows in Dislog:

boundingnode(Node name, type of discourse structure), as in:

```
boundingNode(paragraph, argument).
```

Repair Rules

Although relatively unusual, annotation errors may occur. This is in particular the case when (1) a rule has a fuzzy or ambiguous ending condition w.r.t. the text being processed or (2) when rules of different discourse functions overlap, leading to closing tags that may not be correctly inserted.

In argument recognition, we have indeed some forms of competition between a conclusion and its support which share common linguistic marks. For example, when there are several causal connectors in a sentence the beginning of a support is ambiguous since most supports are introduced by a causal connector. In addition to using concurrent processing strategies, repair rules can resolve errors efficiently, in the same spirit as those developed for Tree adjoining Grammars in (Lopez 1999).

Formally, the most frequent situation is the following:

```
<a>, .., <b> </a>, ... , </b>
```

which must be rewritten into:

```
<a>, ... </a>, ... <b>, ... </b> .
```

This is realized by the following rule:

```
correction([<A> G1 </A> G2 <B> G3 </B>]) -->
    [<A>], gap(G1),[<B>], gap(G2), [</A>], gap(G3), [</B>].
```

The Dislog formalism allows to specify any kind of correction rule. These rules have the same format as those used to identify discourse functions. In our example A and B are variables that stand for any tag, possibly with attributes, not given here for the sake of readability.

Rule Concurrency Management

The current <TextCoop> engine is close to the Prolog execution schema. However, to properly manage rule execution, the properties of discourse structures and the way they are usually organized, we introduce additional constraints, which are, for most of them, borrowed from sentence syntax.

Within a cluster of rules, the execution order is the rule reading order, from the first to the last one. Then, elementary discourse functions are first identified and then bound to others to form larger units, via selective binding rules. Following the principle that a text unit has one and only one discourse function (but may be bound to several other structures via several rhetorical relations) and because rules can be ambiguous from one cluster to another, the order in which rule clusters are executed is a very crucial parameter.

To handle this problem, Dislog requires that rule clusters are executed in a precise, predefined order, implemented in a ***cascade of clusters of rules***. This notion was introduced by (Stabler 1992) with the notion of layers and folding-unfolding mechanisms in an implementation of Generative Syntax theory in Logic Programming.

For example if, in a procedure, we want first titles, then prerequisites and then instructions to be identified, the following constraint must be specified:

```
title < prerequisite < instruction.
```

Since titles have almost the same structure than instructions, but with additional features (bold font, html specific tags, etc.), this prevents titles from being erroneously identified as instructions.

Similarly, it is much preferable to process argument supports, which are easier to identify, before argument conclusions. Processing advice before warnings also limits risks of ambiguities:

```
advice-support < advice-conclusion < warning-support
                                  < warning-conclusion.
```

In the current version of the search engine, there is no backtracking between clusters. Next, when there is no a priori complete order between clusters, those not mentioned in the cascade are executed at the end of the process.

In relation with this notion of cascade, it is possible to declare ***closed zones***, e.g.:

```
closed_zone([title]).
```

indicates that the textual span recognized as a title must not be considered again to recognize other functions within or over it (via a gap). In this example, there will be no further attempt to recognize any discourse structure within a title.

Structural constraints

Let us now consider basic structural principles, which are very common in language syntax. This allows us to contrast the notion of consistuency with the notion of relation in discourse. Consistuency is basically a part-of relation applied to language structures (nouns are parts of NPs) while discourse is basically relational.

Let us introduce here dominance and precedence constraints. Discourse abound in various types of constraints, which may be domain, style or structure dependent (Barenfanger et al. 2006). Dislog can accommodate the specification of a number of such structural constraints.

Dominance constraints are stated as follows:

```
dom(instruction, condition).
```

This constraint states that a conditional expression is always dominated by an instruction. This means that a condition must always be part of an instruction (it is a constituent of that instruction), it cannot stand in a discourse relation with an instruction. In that case, there is no discourse link between a condition and an instruction, the implicit structure being consistuency: a condition is a constituent, or a part of, an instruction.

Similarly, ***non-dominance constraints*** can be stated to ensure that two discourse functions appear in different branches of a discourse representation, e.g.:

```
not_dom(instruction, warning).
```

states that an instruction cannot dominate a warning. However, a warning may be associated with an instruction via a rhetorical relation if its scope is that instruction. This is implemented by a selective binding rule.

Finally, ***precedence constraints*** may be introduced. We only consider here the case of immediate linear precedence, for example:

```
prec(elaborated, elaboration).
```

This constraints indicates that an elaboration must immediately follow what is elaborated. This is a useful constraint for the cases where a nucleus must necessarily precede its satellite: it contributes to the efficiency of the selective binding mechanism and resolves some recognition ambiguities.

Introducing Reasoning Aspects into Discourse Analysis

Discourse relation identification often require some forms of knowledge and reasoning. This is in particular the case to resolve ambiguities in relation identification when there are several candidates or to clearly identify the text span at stake. While some situations are extremely difficult to resolve, others can be processed e.g. via lexical inference or reasoning over ontological knowledge. This problem is very vast and largely open, with exploratory studies e.g. reported in (Van Dijk 1980), (Kintsch 1988), and more recently some debates reported in: http://www.discourses.org/UnpublishedArticles/SpecDis\&Know.htm.

Dislog allows the introduction of reasoning, and the <TextCoop> platform make it possible to integrate knowledge and functions to access knowledge.

Within our perspective, let us give a simple motivational example. The utterance (found in our corpus):

... red fruit tart (strawberries, raspberries) are made ...

contains a structure*: (strawberries, raspberries)* which is ambiguous in terms of discourse functions: it can be an elaboration or an illustration, furthermore the identification of its kernel is ambiguous:

red fruit tart, red fruit ?

A straightforward access to an ontology of fruits indicates that those berries are red fruits, therefore:

- the unit (*strawberries, raspberries)* is interpreted as an illustration, since no new information is given (otherwise it would have been an elaboration)
- its kernel is the *red fruit* unit only.

Note that these two constituents, which must be bound, are not adjacent.

Very informally, the binding rule that binds an illustration with the illustrated text span can be defined as follows, assuming that these are all NPs, with well-identified semantic types:

```
Illustrate -->
  <illustrated>, NP(Type), </illustrated>, gap(G),
  <illustration> NP1(Type1), NP2(Type2), </illustration>,
  [subsume(Type,Type1), subsume(Type, Type2)]
```

The subsume control makes sure that the type of the illustrated element (Type) is more general than the type of the elements in the illustration (Type1, Type2).

The relation between an argument conclusion and its support may not necessarily be straightforward to identify and may involve various types of domain and common-sense knowledge:

Do not park your car at night near this bar: it may cost you fortunes.

Women's living standards have progressed in Nepal: we now see long lines of young girls early morning with their school bags. (Nepali Times).

In this latter example, *school bag* means going to school, then *school* means education, which in turn means better living standards.

Processing Complex Constructions: The Case of Dislocation

As in any language situation, there are complex situations where discourse segments that form larger units may overlap or be shared by several discourse relations. Similarly to syntax, we identified in relatively "free style" texts (i.e. not as controlled as technical procedures, where this should be avoided) phenomena similar to quasi-scrambling situations, free-structure ordering or cleft constructions. This is in particular the case for arguments which are semantically complex constructs, subject to syntactic variations due to pragmatic considerations such as focus or foregrounding. These issues are "deep" syntactic discourse problems that need to be appropriately explained and modelled in Dislog.

As an illustration, let us consider a relatively frequent situation that we call ***dislocation***, which is somewhat close to dislocated constructions in syntax (Lasnik et al. 1988), which occurs when, in a two segment construction, one segment is embedded into the other, as in:

strawberries and raspberries are red fruits, for example

"red fruits" is the kernel of the relation while the illustration is split into two parts: *"strawberries and raspberries"* and *"for example"*. Here the kernel is included into the satellite.

In the following example:

Products X and Y, because of their toxicity, are not allowed in this building.

the support of the argument is embedded into its conclusion, probably to add some stress on the toxicity of these products.

To model this construction, as a first experimentation, in particular to evaluate over-recognition problems and the non-determinism introduced in the parsing, constructions subject to dislocation must be declared as follows:

```
dislocation(argument_conclusion, argument_support, argument).
```

where the first two arguments of this predicate are the two structures subject to dislocation, the second being the embedded one, while the third argument refers to the discourse structure that should bind these two structures.

The constraints are the following:

- the embedded construction is not further dislocated, i.e. it is in a single text segment,
- the construction that embeds the other one is required to be in only two parts, and each segment, the right and the left one, must be recognized by at least one terminal or non-terminal symbol.
- gap symbols cannot range over the embedded structure: they must be fully processed on one sub-segment only.
- the selective binding operation is directly realized from these two segments: these are bound to the type of the third argument of the dislocation predicate without any further control.

From a processing point of view, the <TextCoop> engine attempts to recognize the embedded structure first, then, if no unique text segment can be found for the embedding structure (standard case), it non-deterministically decomposes the rules describing the embedding structure one after the other, following the above constraints, and attempts to recognize it "around" the embedded one.

Finally, we observed in our corpora quasi-scrambling situations, a simple case being the illustration relation. Consider again the example above, which can also be written as follows:

strawberries are red fruits similarly to raspberries, for example

where the enumeration itself is subject to dislocation. Obviously, such a construction must be avoided in technical texts.

The <TextCoop> Architecture and Environment

The architecture of <TextCoop> is rather standard. It is organized around the following modules:

- a module of rules or patterns written in Dislog. This module includes the various types of rules recognizing basic discourse functions and the binding rules,
- one or more modules dedicated to lexical resources. It is advised to have different modules for general purpose lexical data and lexical data specific to certain discourse constructs. This allows an easier management of lexical data and a better update and re-use over various applications,
- a module dedicated to morphological processing
- a module for the management of the system: this module includes the management of constraints and the cascade specification.
- the <TextCoop> engine, developed below, which is associated with a few utilities (Prolog basic functions, input/output management, character encoding management, etc.).

These elements are given in the freeware archive which can be obtained upon request to the author.

In a second stage, we defined a working environment for <TextCoop> in order to help the grammar writer to develop applications. This environment is in a very early stage of development: many more experiments are needed before reaching a stable analysis of the needs. Accessing already defined and formatted resources is of much interest for authors.

The following sets of resources are available for French and English:

- lists of connectors, organized by general types: temporal, causal, concession, etc. (Miltasaki et al. 2004) developed an original learning method to classify connectors and related marks,
- list of specific terms which are typical of discourse functions, e.g.: terms specific of illustration, summarization, reformulation, etc.

- lists of verbs organized by semantic classes, close to those found in WordNet, which have been adapted or refined for discourse analysis, with a focus e.g. on propositional attitude verbs, report verbs, (Wierzbicka 1987),
- list of terms with positive or negative polarity, essentially adjectives, but also some nouns and verbs. This is useful in particular to evaluate the strength of arguments,
- local grammars for e.g.: temporal expressions, expression of quantity, etc.,
- some already defined modules of discourse function rules to recognize general purpose discourse functions such as illustration, definition, reformulation, goal and condition.
- some predefined functions and predicates to access knowledge and control features (e.g. subsumption),
- morphosyntactic tagging functions,
- some basic utilities for integrating knowledge (e.g. ontologies) into the environment.

This environment is compatible with sentence parsers which can operate on the text independently of the tags, or within tag fields. Some of the elements of this environment are illustrated in the next chapter.

The <TextCoop> Engine

Let us now introduce the way the <TextCoop> engine runs. More details on the way it is implemented are given in Chapter 5. The engine and its environment are implemented in SWI Prolog, using the standard Prolog syntax without referring to any libraries to guarantee readability, ease of update and portability. It is therefore a stand-alone application.

A major principle is that the declarative character of constraints and structure building is preserved in the system. The engine, implemented in Prolog, interprets them at the appropriate control points.

The engine follows the cascade specification for the execution of rule clusters. Within each cluster, rules are activated in their reading order, one after the other. Backtracking manages rule failures. If a rule in a rule cluster succeeds on a given text span, then the other possibilities for that cluster are not considered (but rules of other clusters may be considered in a later stage of the cascade).

A priori, the text is processed via a left to right strategy. However, <TextCoop> offers a right to left strategy for rules where the most relevant marks are to the right of the rule, in order to limit backtracking. For the two types of readings, the system is tuned to recognize the smallest text span that satisfies the rule structure.

The engine can work on different textual units: sentences, paragraphs, sections, etc. depending on the kind of structure or phenomenon to recognize (some have a very large scope such as the "frame" relation that constrains a whole paragraph or even more, while others such as the goal of an instruction or an illustration usually operate over a single sentence. "Title" relations also range over a large text fragment).

Relevant units can be specified in the cascade for each cluster of rules. The system is more efficient and generates less ambiguities with smaller units. It processes raw text, html or XML texts. A priori, the initial XML structure of the processed document is preserved.

The code associated with the <TextCoop> engine is rather small. We present here its main features. It is based on the notion of meta-interpreter in Prolog. In a meta-interpreter, different processing strategies can be developed besides the top-down, left-to-right strategy offered in Prolog.

Before developing a few details concerning the <TextCoop> engine, let us consider, as an introduction, a meta-interpreter of Definite Clause Grammar rules (DCGs). Most Prolog versions automatically translate DCGs into Prolog. However, designing a meta-interpreter can be useful e.g. to change the processing strategy.

Let us assume that a DCG rule is represented as:

```
Axiom --> Body.
```

and a lexical entry as:

```
Axiom --> [Word].
```

Axiom and Body may have any kind of structure (term with arguments, feature structure, etc.). The clause parse that enables the processing of the grammar rule format given above is defined as follows. The two first arguments respectively manage the input and output list of words (corresponding to a sentence) to process:

```
:-op(1100,xfy,-->).   % definition of the priority of the operator -->

parse(X, X1, Axiom) -->
  (Axiom --> Body),              % if unification with Axiom
  parse(X, X1, Body), !.         %  succeeds then process the Body
parse([M|X], X, [M]) :- !.       % processes lexical entry
parse(X, X1, (C1, C2)) :-        % Body processing from left to right
  parse(X, X2, C1),
  parse(X2, X1, C2).             % Body = (C1, (C2))
```

To implement a right-to-left processing strategy, useful for example for languages where the head is to the right, the only modification is to change the order C1 and C2 are processed as follows:

```
parse(X, X1, (C1, C2)) :-          % Body processing from right to left
  parse(X2, X1, C2),
  parse(X, X2, C1).
```

Let us now consider the main features of the <TextCoop> engine. More details on the rule format and on how to launch the system are given in the next chapter. The general form of a rule is:

```
forme(Name,
        Input string,
        Output string,
        [right hand side symbols in the rule],
        Reasoning terms,
        Result).
```

The main rule of the meta-interpreter is then:

```
corr(Forme,E,S,C):-  %recognizes the rule "Forme" in the sequence E-S
                      % result is stored in C (annotated text in general,
  forme(Forme,E,S, [A1| F1], Re, C),
                     % call to a rule according to the cascade
  typeOK(A1,E,S1),
          % checks whether the first symbol in the rule, A1, is found
  suiteOK(S1,S,F1),             % next steps till the end of the rule
  dominanceFinOK(Forme,S),     % dominance controls
          % in case of failure of the above terms, there is backtracking
  executer(Re),                % processing of the reasoning aspects.
  non_dominance(Forme,C).      % non dominance control.
```

System Performances

Let us now analyze the performances of <TextCoop> with respect to relevant linguistic dimensions, and contrast these with performances of parsers dedicated to sentence processing.

General Results

The <TextCoop> engine and related data are implemented in SWI Prolog which runs on a number of environments (Windows, Linux, Apple). Other versions of Prolog (such as Sicstus may not contain all the built-in predicates used in our utility file). Our implementation can support a multi-threaded communication with external devices. This has been tested with the <TextCoop> engine embedded into a Java environment in collaboration with the Prometil company. This is useful for example to implement a "parallel" processing on several machines or to distribute e.g. lexical data, grammars and domain knowledge on various machines for large scale or real-time applications.

The <TextCoop> engine has been relatively optimized and some recommendations for developing large sets of rules have been produced in order to allow a reasonable efficiency.

For the evaluation given below, our basis is a test application with a lexicon of 1300 words and a set of 78 rules defined in Chapter 2 and related to procedure processing. The test system recognizes 8 different structures (or a subset of them): instructions, warnings, advice, prerequisites, goals, conditions, illustrations and circumstances. In the next chapter, more relations are considered. This test application is purely linguistic, it does not use any external source of knowledge to solve ambiguities. The system runs on a standard PC with Windows 7, an average volume of 18 Megabytes (Mb, hereafter) of text is processed per hour.

Results are discussed in more depth below: they give a better view on the performances of the system. An important feature is the type of text which is processed. Indeed, professional texts, because of their very regular form, possibly following authoring recommendations, produce much better results that dirty texts such as those coming from the web. However, we also observed large differences in quality and homogeneity in professional texts which make evaluation results somewhat relative.

Lexical Issues

An important feature of discourse structure recognition is that most of the lexical resources which are needed are generic. This means that the system can be deployed almost on any application domain without any major lexical changes. This result characterizes a number of discourse relations whose recognition is based on a small set of predefined linguistic marks and structures.

More precisely, in terms of lexical resources, the following main categories are used for technical document analysis:

(1) closed classes: discourse connectors, negation, pronouns, prepositions and some basic icons and forms of punctuation and

typography. A number of them are given as illustration in Chapter 2.

(2) open classes: common classes of verbs (e.g. communication and change of state verbs (about 600 verbs for French)), action verbs and nouns, verbs and some adjectives with a strong positive or negative polarity (currently 360 terms for French, slightly less for English).

In our applications on procedural text processing, instructions require the recognition of action verbs, which is quite large a set in general (about 10 000 verbs for French, more for English). To overcome this difficulty, we specialize the action verb lexicon to a given application domain: this is the main lexical tuning which is needed to deploy a system on a specific domain.

It should be noted that even for a small domain like cooking, the number of verbs is about 350. For gardening and do-it-yourself, this number is about 700 verbs. In professional procedures, this number is much lower, between 50 and 150 for a given activity. This is essentially due to the influence of authoring recommendations (Chapter 3). The same remark holds for most types of open lexical resources. In total, the average size of the required lexical resources (number of rules being fixed) for discourse processing for an application such as procedural text parsing on a given domain is around 900 words, which is very small compared to what is necessary to process the structure of sentences for the same domain. Results below are given for French. Results for English are a priori comparable.

The following table reports the system performances depending on the lexicon size. These sizes correspond to real and comprehensive lexicons for a given domain (e.g. 400 corresponds to the cooking domain, the case with 180 lexical entries is a toy system):

Lexicon size	**Mega-Bytes of text / hour**
180	39
400	27
900	20
1400	18
2000	17

Table 4-1 Performances according to lexical size

These results are somewhat difficult to precisely analyse, since they depend on the number of words by syntactic category, the way they are coded and the order in which they are listed in the lexicon (in relation with the Prolog processing strategy). In order to limit some complexity related to morphological analysis, a crucial aspect for Romance languages, a preliminary tagging process has been carried out to limit backtracking. The way lexical resources are used in rules is also a parameter which is difficult to precisely analyse.

Globally, reducing the size of the lexicon to those elements which are really needed for the application allows a clear, but moderate, increase in the system performances. This is particularly true for small size lexicons, which are those required for industrial applications. This means some lexical tuning, but on a limited scale.

Issues related to the rule system size and complexity

Two parameters related to the rule system are investigated here: how much the number of rules and the rule size impact the efficiency. The results obtained concerning the total number of rules in the grammar at stake are the following:

Number of rules	Mega-Bytes of text / hour
20	29
40	23
70	19
90	18

Table 4-2 Performances according to the number of rules

As can be noted, increasing the number of rules has a moderate impact on performances, one of the reasons is that the most prototypical rules are in general specified first and therefore executed first. Rules considered here have an average complexity: 4 symbols and a gap in average, and an average of 8 rules per cluster. Lexical size here is fixed (500 entries). 20 rules is a very small system while 80 to 120 rules is a standard size for an application.

The results we obtain are difficult to accurately analyze: besides rule ordering considerations, results depend on the distribution of rules per cluster and on the form of the rules. For example, the presence of non-ambiguous linguistic marks at the beginning of a rule enhances rule selection, and therefore improves efficiency.

Constraints such as those presented above on page 85 are also very costly since they are checked at each step of the parsing process for the structures at stake. This means a lot of computation over possibly long text spans or large structures.

Finally, selective binding rules have little impact on efficiency: their first symbol being an XML tag, backtracking occurs at an early stage of the rule inspection.

Let us now consider the rule size impact (number of symbols, whatever they are, per rule), which is obviously an important feature, in particular the number of gaps is crucial:

Rule complexity	Mega-Bytes of text / hour
3	30
4	23
5	20
7	18

Table 4-3 Performances according to the rule average complexity

With the number of rules and the size of the lexicon being kept fixed, we note also that the rule size has a moderate impact on performances, slightly higher than the number of rules. This may be explained by the fact that the symbols starting the rules are, in a number of cases, sufficiently well differentiated to provoke early backtracking if the rule is not the one that will succeed. If we consider the rule samples given in Chapter 2, we indeed note that crucial elements such as connectors often appear very early in the rules.

However, the number of lexical entries associated with these symbols may have an important impact. If the symbol is a specific type of connector or, conversely, if it is a noun or a verb, then this may entail substantial efficiency differences. This is difficult however to precisely evaluate at this stage. Finally, note that rules dedicated to explanation have in general between 4 and 6 symbols including gaps.

Comparison of Efficiency with Sentence Processing

Globally, we can conclude that there is an impact on efficiency in what concerns the size of the lexicon, the number of rules and their complexity. However, from a toy system to a real size application the impact is about a factor of 5 to 8, which is moderate. For the reasons advocated above, the system is not very sensitive to the size of the rule system.

Although we do not have precise figures for comparable treatments, these performances substantially contrast with sentence parsers where complexity does increase very much with the number of rules, and to a lesser extend with the size of the lexicon. This being said, there are major differences between sentence and discourse processing which justifies these differences:

- although this depends on the syntactic theory adopted, in general, sentence parsers based on rules have a larger number of rules (a few hundred), and these rules are often recursive, our system has a priori a lower number of rules,
- in contrast, discourse processing requires rules which are not recursive, structures being constructed by selective binding rules (about three rules per discourse structure) which form an autonomous system,
- sentence processing requires in general much more lexical resources and an extensive morphological analysis, this is more limited in the case of discourse,
- sentences in real documents being complex, most parsers are shallow parsers, which can process substructures instead of the whole structure if it cannot be recognized. Then substructures are either left as such or bound by means of various relations such as dependencies,
- discourse processing rules are based on a few, recurrent, linguistic marks, what is in between these symbols (gaps) is of little interest for discourse rules: this allows a comprehensive bottom-up parsing where complete structures can be recognized.

Conclusion

In this chapter, we have presented the foundational aspects of Dislog and the features offered by this logic-based programming language to process discourse structures. Then we have introduced the <TextCoop> platform on which Dislog runs. We have outlined in this chapter the linguistic architecture of this platform and have illustrated the way it runs in Prolog via a meta-interpreter. Finally, we have presented and discussed performance issues which are crucial since processing the discourse structure of texts is in general not very efficient due to the size of a text and to the complexity and ambiguity of discourse structures.

In the chapter that follows, we first show how to use the <TextCoop> platform in a very concrete way, based on the freeware archive which is available from the author. In Chapter 2 we have presented a methodology for authoring rules and lexical data and a large variety of types of discourse processing rules related to explanation. Chapter 6 is devoted to a specific type of technical document: requirements. Finally, Chapter 7 describes the main elements of the Lelie project which makes an intensive use of the principles described here.

CHAPTER FIVE

PROGRAMMING IN DISLOG

PATRICK SAINT-DIZIER

In this chapter, the use of <TextCoop> and Dislog is explained in detail. This chapter has essentially a practical purpose, it is a kind of user manual. It is of interest to the reader who wants to develop applications, otherwise it can be skipped. The TextCoop archive can be obtained from the author (stdizier@irit.fr), it is freely available for research and training purposes. In this chapter, we first describe how to install TextCoop from the archive. Next, we develop principles and a simple method to write Dislog rules so that the reader can start writing simple rules. Finally, we show how rules such as those given in Chapter 2 are implemented in Dislog, including the implementation of lexical resources and the specification of constraints. Detailed comments are given so that the reader can define himself his own rules or write variants of the examples which are given.

Using Dislog and <TextCoop>

Let us first show how <TextCoop> and Dislog can be installed from the archive and how to run a Dislog programme.

Installation

<TextCoop> is a meta-interpreter which is implemented in Prolog. To make the system portable, only the kernel syntax of Prolog is used, therefore, most versions of Prolog using the Edinburgh syntax should allow <TextCoop> to run adequately (possibly a few predefined predicates will need to be revised if a Prolog implementation such as Sicstus is used). We recommend to use SWI Prolog, which is free and runs efficiently on several platforms. Note that SWI Prolog seems to run faster on a Linux environment than on MS Windows.

The only thing you have to do is to unzip the <TextCoop> archive into a directory of your choice. A priori it is simpler to keep all the files in a single directory. However, the text files you analyse can be stored in another directory. Basically, the archive contains two directories, one for the French version and the other one for the English version (files end by Fr or Eng depending on the language).

Each directory contains the following files:

- the engine: textcoopV4.pl
- a specific file for user declarations and parameters: decl.pl
- a set of basic functions that you do not need to update or even look at: fonctions.pl
- a set of lexicons that contain various types of data: lexiqueBase.pl, lexSpecialise.pl, lexiqueIllustr.pl. You can obviously construct several additional lexicons, but you must add the call to their compilation at the beginning of the textcoopV4.pl file. The French version also contains a list of categorized verbs (eeeaccents.pl). It must be noted that all the rules corresponding to a specific predicate must be defined in the same file
- a file with rules or patterns: rules.pl
- a toy file with "local" grammar samples written in DCG format: gram.pl
- a file for the input-output operations: es.pl and another one for reading files of various text formats and transforming them into Prolog: lire.pl
- a few files to run and test the system: demo.txt, after processing a text file, the system produces two output files: demo-out.html (tags, no colours for further processing) and demo-c-out.html (same thing but with colours and spaces to facilitate reading). However, note that we have not developed at this stage any user interface
- additional files can be added, for example to include knowledge or specific reasoning procedures. Nothing is included at this level in this beta version.

Starting

There are several ways to read and modify your files and to call Prolog. Emacs and similar editors are particularly well-adapted. We recommend the use of Editplus V3 for those who do not have any preference. Prolog can be launched directly from the editor and the code, or selected parts of it, can be easily re-interpreted when modifications are made. It is important to keep in mind that text files encoded in the UTF8 or UTF16 formats may be problematic for Prolog, which basically takes as input texts under an ISO format. Character encoding may be tuned in some environments, such as in Linux. It is recommended that the texts you want to analyse are all in .txt format.

To start the system, you must launch Prolog from your environment, e.g. from Editplus. You must then "consult" your file(s). Since the file textcoopV4.pl contains consult orders for all the other files, you just need to consult it, via the menu of the Prolog window, or, in the window by typing:

['textcoopV4.pl'].

care about ERROR messages, but you can ignore warnings.

Then to launch TextCoop, type the main call:

annotF.

then you are required to enter your file name, between quotes, ended by a dot, as usual in Prolog:

?- 'demo.txt'.

The system processes the text and you will then see the display on your screen of a large number of intermediate files which are created and re-used. Each cycle of these intermediate files corresponds to the execution of a cluster of rules given in the rule cascade. Results are stored in two files: demo-out.html (html tags, no colour) and demo-c-out.html (same thing but with colours and spaces to facilitate reading).

The file es.pl contains a few other input/output calls that you may wish to explore. You can also change the display colours in this file, or add or withdraw the display of some tags. The contents of the tags are produced by discourse analysis rules, described in the "Representation" argument.

Writing Rules in Dislog

Rules are stored in this archive in the rules.pl file. These rules have been produced from a manual analysis of linguistic phenomena, they could have been the result of a statistical analysis. A priori, the Dislog language is flexible enough to accept a large variety of forms. A number of rules related to explanation in technical documents are presented in Chapter 2, together with a number of examples to which the reader can refer. Elements of a simple methodology for designing rules are given below in the chapter to facilitate rule authoring.

The first thing to do if you want to analyse a discourse structure is to define and characterize the phenomena to treat via a linguistic analysis.

This means a corpus analysis, then abstracting over corpus observations using grammar symbols and generalizing these abstractions at an appropriate linguistic level. The next stages are to develop the lexical resources (cues typical of the structure being investigated and other useful resources) and write rules, following the syntax given in Chapter 2. These rules must then be encoded in Dislog, where a few more arguments and formatting issues must be considered, as explained in a section at the end of this chapter.

Let us first take an example on how to write Dislog rules. The rule that describes a purpose satellite (Chapter 2) can be written in an external format as follows:

```
purpose -->
  connector(goal),
  verb([action,impinf]),
  gap(G),
  punctuation.
```

e.g, where the purpose clause is underlined:

To write a good essay on English literature*, you need to do five things, first start [...].*

This rule says that a purpose satellite is composed of a connector of type goal, followed by an action verb in the imperative or infinitive form followed by a gap. The structure ends by a punctuation mark. Labels such as goal, impinf or action are defined by the rule author, they are not imposed by the system. These tags may be encoded in a variety of ways: as lists (as in this example) or as a feature structure. It is preferable to have all the features stored in a single argument.

As presented in Chapter 4, the general form of a rule coded in Dislog is:

```
forme(LHS, E, S, RuleBody, Constraints, Result).
```

where:

- **LHS** is the symbol on the left-hand side of the rule. It is the name of the cluster of rules representing the various structures corresponding to a phenomenon (e.g. purpose satellites). It is used in various constraints and in the cascade to refer to this cluster.
- **E and S** are respectively the input and output strings representing the sentence or text to process, similarly to the DCGs difference list notation. The informal meaning is that between E and S there is a purpose clause. E and S are lists of words coded in Prolog.
- **RuleBody** is the right-hand part of the rule, it is described below,
- **Constraints** is a list that contains a variety of constraints to check. They may also be calls to knowledge and reasoning procedures

which are written in Prolog and automatically executed at the end of the rule. An empty list means that there is no constraints. It is always evaluated to true.

- **Result** denotes the result which includes the string of words of the input structure with tags included at the appropriate places. Tags in rules may include variables.

The rule body is encoded as follows. Each grammar symbol has four arguments (this is a choice which can be modified, but seems optimal and easy to use):

name(String,Feature,E,S).

where:

- **String** denotes the String which is reproduced in the result in conjunction with tags. In general it is the string that has been read for that symbol (e.g. the difference between E and S), but it can be any other form (e.g. a normalized form, a reordered string, etc.).
- **Feature** is the argument that contains information about the symbol, encoded e.g. as a list of values or as a typed feature structure. The format is unconstrained, but the rule writer must manage it.
- **E** and **S** are respectively the input and output lists of words, as above, for the analysis of this particular symbol. E and S form what is called the difference list in logic-grammars.

Gap symbols have a different format:

gap(NotSkipped,Stop,E,S,Skipped).

where:

- **NotSkipped** is a list of symbols which must not be skipped before the gap stops. If it finds such a symbol, then the gap fails. So far, this list is limited to a single symbol for efficiency reasons. We have not found so many cases where multiple restrictions are needed. If really needed, these must be coded in the "gap" clause.
- **Stop** is a list: [Symbol, Restrictions] that describes where the gap must stop: it must stop immediately before it finds a symbol Symbol with the restrictions Restrictions. In general this is the explicit symbol that follows the gap in the rule, but this is not compulsory.
- **E** and **S** are as above,
- **Skipped** is the difference between E and S, namely the sequence of words that have been skipped by the gap.

It must be noted that a gap must only appear in a rule between two explicit symbols. While processing a rule, if a gap reaches the end of a sentence (or a predefined ending mark such as a dot) without having found the symbol that follows in the rule, then it fails and the rule also fails.

The symbol skip is slightly different from the gap symbol. It allows the parser to skip a maximum number of N words given as parameter. It has the same structure as a gap, except that the second argument is an integer (in general small) that indicates the maximum number of words to skip:

```
skip(NotSkipped, Number, E, S, Skipped).
```

The symbol in the rule that immediately follows a skip symbol defines the termination of the skip. It is not specified in the skip symbol. If the maximum number of words to be skipped is not followed by the expected symbol, then the skip fails.

The rule given above for a purpose satellite then translates as follows in Dislog:

```
forme(purpose-eng,
E, S,
[ connector(CONN,goal,E,E1),
  verb(V,[action,impinf],E1,E2),
  gap([],[ponct,_],E2,E3,Saute1),
  ponct(Ponct,_,E3,S)],
 [],
['<purpose>', CONN, V, Saute1, '</purpose>', Ponct ]).}
```

This rule is represented as a Prolog fact so that the TextCoop meta-interpreter can read it and then process it. The reader can note the sequences of input-output variables E-E1-E2-E3-S used as in DCGs. The last argument encodes the result, for example the way the original sentence is tagged. Tags may be inserted at any place; they may contain variables elaborated in the inference (also called Constraints) field. In fact, a priori any form of representation can be produced in this field. The above example shows that the result is produced in a very declarative and readable way.

Symbols in a rule can be marked as optional or can appear several times. This is respectively encoded using the operators opt and plus applied to grammar symbols:

```
forme(purpose-eng,
E, S,
[ connector(CONN,goal,E,E1),
 opt(verb(V,[action,impinf],E1,E2)),
 gap([],[ponct,_],E2,E3,Saute1),
 ponct(Ponct,_,E3,S)],
 [],
['<purpose>', CONN, V, Saute1, '</purpose>', Ponc ]).
```

In this example, the verb is indicated as optional: if it is not found, then the gap starts immediately after the connector. If there is no verb, the variable V in the result field is not instantiated and does not produce any result in the last argument (variables are ignored in the representation sequence since their contents is empty).

In the example below, a sequence of auxiliaries is allowed between the connector and the verb:

```
forme(purpose-eng,
E, S,
[ connector(CONN,goal,E,E1),
  plus(aux(Aux,_,E1,E2),
  verb(V,[action,_],E2,E3),
  gap([],[ponct,_],E3,E4,Saute1),
  ponct(Ponct,_,E4,S)],
 [],
['<purpose>', CONN, Aux, V, Saute1, '</purpose>', Ponc ]).
```

The operators plus and opt are defined in the kernel of <TextCoop> and are implemented in the textcoopV4.pl file. These operators can be modified and variants can be implemented without affecting the remainder of the system. For example a predicate plus2 that would require at least two instances of the symbol it includes could easily be added to the <TextCoop> engine.

Finally, as the reader can note it, the transformation of rules written in the external format into the Dislog internal format obeys very regular and strict principles. Similarly to e.g. DCGs, it is possible, but however more complex than for DCGs, to write a few lines of code in Prolog that produce such an internal form from the external one.

Writing Context-Dependent Rules

A closer look at the Dislog rule formalism shows that it is possible to use this formalism to implement context-dependent rules. In fact, the left-hand side symbol, the cluster name, can be viewed as an identifier, and the power of the rule formalism can be shifted to the pair left-hand part (RuleBody) and representation or right-hand part or the rule (Result). The left-hand part is indeed often the input form to identify and its relation with the Result introduces a large diversity of treatments.

We already advocated the case of binding rules, which are clearly type 1 if not type 0 rules. It is possible in Dislog to develop any other kind of rules, e.g. to realize structure transformation with some form of context sensitivity.

To illustrate this point, let us consider again the example given in Chapter 2 that deals with the binding of a warning conclusion with its support. The following rule:

```
Warning -->
<warning-concl>,gap(G1),</warning-concl>, gap(G2),
<warning-supp>, gap(G3),  </warning-supp>, gap(G4), eos.
```

binds a warning conclusion with a warning support. The result is a warning, represented by the following XML structure:

```
<warning>
<warning-concl>,G1,</warning-concl>, G2,
<warning-supp>, G3,  </warning-supp>, G4,
</warning>.
```

The same type of rule can be written to bind any kernel with its satellite, or more complex structures, e.g. a title (denoting an action to realize) with its prerequisites and instructions.

Parameters and Structure Declarations

In contrast with Prolog, but with the aim of improving efficiency, it is necessary in Dislog to declare a few elements, among which non-terminal symbols. This is realized in the decl.pl file. A number of standard symbols are already declared, but check that yours are declared; otherwise the rules that contain these symbols will fail.

First, in order to enable a proper variable binding, any symbol used in rules must be declared as follows:

```
tt(adv(Mot,Restr,E,S), E,S).
tt(adj(Mot,Restr,E,S), E,S).
tt(neg(Mot,Restr,E,S), E,S).
tt(np(Mot,Restr,E,S), E,S).
tt(det(Mot,Restr,E,S), E,S).
etc.
```

In this example, the symbols adv, adj, neg, np and det are declared. The co-occurrence of the symbols E and S allows us to bind the variables of the symbols (adv, adj, etc.) with the string of words to process in the meta-interpreter (the <TextCoop> engine).

Similarly, any symbol which can be optional must be declared by means of a piece of code. The code must be reproduced from the following example which encodes optionality for auxiliaries:

```
opt(aux(AUX,A,E1,E2)) :-
    aux(AUX,A,E1,E2), !.
opt(aux([],_,E,E)).
```

A similar declaration is necessary for multiple occurrences:

```
plus(adv(T,_,E1,S)) :-
  adv(T1,_,E1,E2), !,
  plus(adv(T2,_,E2,S)),
  conc(T,S,E1).
 plus(adv(T,_,S,S)).
```

This portion of code must be duplicated for all relevant symbols.

Instead of writing these declarations, a higher-order encoding could have been implemented, but it does affect efficiency quite substantially. In a future version of the system (V5), an alternative solution will be found so that this constraint is no longer necessary. Some of these declarations could be automated from the grammar, but they may impose additional rule format constraints that rule authors may not want to have.

Constraints presented in Chapter 4 must also be declared (at least one instance of each type must be present in the code to avoid failures), a few examples are provided here:

```
exclut_unite(title).

termin(['<',condition,'>'],['<','/',condition,'>']).
termin(['<',purpose,'>'],['<','/',purpose,'>']).
termin(['<',circumstance,'>'],['<','/',circumstance,'>']).
termin(['<',restatement,'>'],['<','/',restatement,'>']).

dom(instr-eng,[but, condopt-eng, restatement]).

non_dom(instr-eng,[avt,cons]).
```

A few constraints are given in the decl.pl file as examples. These must be kept to avoid system failures. This file also contains the cascade declaration, as explained below.

Lexical Data

Lexical data is specified in the lexique.pl file. Lexical data can follow the standard categories and features of linguistic theories or be *ad hoc*, depending on situations. Lexical data is given in DCG format (Pereira et al. 1980) (Saint-Dizier 1994). In general, you have to design yourself your own lexicon with its features. In this first version, we simply provide a few examples to help rule authors. However, in addition to those available on the net, we are developing sets of lexical markers and other resources which are useful for discourse analysis. These will be made available in a coming version (V5).

Here are a few examples included into this version:

```
% pronouns
pro([we],_) --> [we].
pro([you],_) --> [you].

 % goal connectors
connector([in,order,to], goal) --> [in,order,to].
connector([in,order,that], goal) --> [in,order,that].
connector([so], goal) --> [so].
connector([so,as,to], goal) --> [so,as,to].

 % specific marks describing the beginning of a sentence
mdeb([debph],_) --> [debph].          % by-default mark internal to the system
mdeb(['<li>'],_) --> ['<',li,'>'].
mdeb([1],_) --> ['-',1].

 % condition
expr([if],cond) --> [if].

 % specific marks for reformulation (no features associated)
expr_reform([in,other,words],_) --> [in,other,words].
expr_reform([to,put,it,another,way],_) --> [to,put,it,another,way].
expr_reform([that,is,to,say],_) --> [that,is,to,say].

 % tag (= balise) represented as lexical data: this is useful for rules
 % which basically bind structures on the basis of already produced tags,
 % each element has a type specified in the second argument.
balise([<, instruction, >],instruction) --> [<, instruction, >].
balise([<, /, instruction, >],endinstruction) --> [<, /, instruction, >].

balise([<, goal, >],goal) --> [<, goal, >].
balise([<,/,goal, >],endgoal) --> [<, /,goal, >].
```

Other Types of Resources

This first version is relatively limited and does not contain so many additional tools and facilities. These will come in the next available version of the tool (version V5). However, version V4 contains the kernel necessary to implement the recognition of most discourse structures and to bind them adequately.

The file gram.pl of the archive contains a few grammar rules written in DCG style. These are compatible with the Dislog symbol formats. Indeed, it is possible to have non-terminal symbols in rules which are associated with a grammar in that module. This is useful for example to capture specific constructions which are better described by means of rules and not simply by lexical entries. Here is a very simple example for noun phrases (np):

```
np([A,B],_,E,S) :-
    det(A,_,E,S1),
    n(B,_,S1,S).
np([A],_,E,S) :-
   pro(A,_,E,S).
```

This short sample of a grammar for noun phrases can be directly called from Dislog rules. Note that the first argument of the np symbols contains the string of words which corresponds to the NP. This argument could include any other form, e.g. a normalized form or a tree. The second argument (features associated with the symbol, left empty here) argument must have the same structure as in the Dislog rules.

Input-Output Management

The management of the input-output files is realized in several files. The main file is es.pl which contains the main calls and dynamically produces names for output and intermediate files (to avoid conflicts between parses). This file contains procedures that produce two kinds of output displays: a file for further processing which is a basic XML file and a similar file where structures get a colour for easier reading. This latter file can be read by most XML editors.

File names are created dynamically from the input file name: demo-out.html (tags, no colours) and demo-c-out.html (tags and colours) for the demo.txt file. If you have sufficient Prolog programming skills, you can modify this file, e.g. changing colours, if you need it.

It is important to note that, in this first version, structure processing is realized on a sentence basis. We have improved and parameterized this situation which is somewhat limited. It will shortly be possible to implement other units besides sentences such as paragraphs. Meanwhile, you can end the text portions you want to process as a single unit by a dot, and replace dots ending sentences in these portions by another symbol, e.g. the word "dot", which can be re-written later by a real dot in the output file.

Basically, input files must be plain text, possibly with XML marks. Word files cannot be processed. It must also be noted that Prolog has some difficulties with UTF8 encoded texts, therefore ISO encodings must be preferred.

The other files for input-output operations are internal to the system and should not be modified: lire.pl reads files under various formats and produces a list of words, which is the entry for the structure processing. In this module, some characters are transformed into words in order to avoid any interference with Prolog predefined elements. These are then restored in their original form when the final output is produced. This is an important issue to keep in mind, since some elements in the lexicon must take these transformations into account.

The module functions.pl contains a variety of basic utilities, which you may use for various purposes besides the present software.

Execution Schema and Structure of Control

The <TextCoop> engine is a meta-interpreter written in standard Prolog. Meta-interpretation is a well-known technique in Logic Programming which is very convenient for developing e.g. alternative processing strategies or demonstrators. It also allows us to realize a fast prototyping. The strategy implemented in <TextCoop> is quite similar to the Prolog strategy. However there are some major differences you need to be aware of.

The <TextCoop> engine considers, for a given text, rule clusters one after the other. Therefore, rule clusters must be organized in a cascade that describes the cluster execution order. The cascade must be declared in the decl.pl file as follows, where eng is the cascade name:

```
cascade(eng,
  [circ-eng,
   condition-eng,
   purpose-eng,
   restate-eng,
    illus-eng]).
```

The whole text is inspected for each rule cluster, one after the other. If a cluster does not produce any result, there is no failure and the next one is activated. In case you wish to define several cascades, you must define additional identifiers. In our example, the first argument of the cascade predicate is its identifier: eng.

During execution, you can see in the Prolog window the different steps of the cascade with the intermediate files being produced and compiled. Several cascades can be used sequentially if needed or relevant (e.g. for modularity purposes or for different types of tasks on a text which are not related).

Within a cluster, rules are considered one after the other, from the first to the last one, similarly to Prolog strategy. However, there is a major difference with Prolog due to Dislog rule format. The string of words to process is traversed from left to right (the code which is in the archive also provides a right to left strategy), at each step (i.e. for each word), the engine attempts to find a rule in that cluster (starting by the first one in the cluster) that would start by this word (via derivation or lexical inspection). If this succeeds, then the rule considered at this point, independently of its position in the cluster, is activated. If the whole rule succeeds, the result is produced (annotated text) and no other rule is considered in that cluster. If the rule fails at some point then backtracking occurs.

For example, consider the following abstract sentence to process:

[a,n,a,d,f,b,c],

and the following (simplified) set of rules:

```
s --> d, f.
s --> a, b.
s --> a, d.
```

When parsing the string, the first a and then the n are considered without any success since there is no s → a, n rule, but then the second occurrence of a is the left-corner of the second and third rules above. The second rule fails since no b is found after a, but the third rule succeeds. Note that in DCGs the first rule would have succeeded with a partial parser because the sentence contains the sequence [d,f], but since it comes later than the sequence [a,d] in the reading order, it does not succeed in Dislog. This strategy favours left-extraposed or left-sensitive structures in case there are several candidates for a sentence. This situation is the most common in discourse analysis, where, in most language, marks such as connectors appear to the left of the structures (Stede 2012).

Note that if the second rule were:

```
s -->
   a, gap, b.
```

then it would have succeeded first on the segment :
[a,n,a,d,f,b]
with gap = [n,a,d,f].

In our approach, when a rule in a cluster succeeds, for efficiency reasons, no other rule in that cluster is considered and there is no backtracking at any further stage in that cluster. For users who want to recognize several occurrences of the same structure in a sentence, it is best to write a complex rule that repeats the structure to find. This is not so elegant, but this limits backtracking and entails a much better efficiency. It is also possible to suppress a cut (noted as !) in the meta-interpreter code, but this is not recommended.

It should be noted that other processing strategies can easily be implemented in <TextCoop>. For example, in the interpreter, we give an example of a right-to-left processing strategy which may be of interest for rules where the relevant tags appear at the end of the rule, i.e. to the right of the rule, although this is quite unusual in discourse analysis. Similarly, it is also possible to write another processing strategy that would proceed rule by rule in a cluster and check whether a rule can be applied at any place in the sentence to process, instead of proceeding word by word and looking for the rule that succeeds the first. This is another strategy, which may be less efficient.

The Art of Writing Dislog Rules

Some readers may remain sceptical on their ability to write rules in Dislog. In fact, our experience shows writing rules is very easy because of the declarative character of Dislog and of logic programmes in general. This is the case here for rules as well as for constraints. A few days of practice should suffice to be able to write rules with a certain degree of sophistication. Some familiarity with Prolog and DCGs is however useful, see (Pereira et al. 1980) and, for a survey, (Saint-Dizier 1994) among others.

The ease of writing rules and the adequacy of the rule formalism with respect to corpus observations are major properties that any rule system must offer. To write well-designed rules, experiments are needed over a large number of domains and applications in particular on the way to identify rules, to generalize them, and to reach a certain level of linguistic adequacy and predictability. Another challenge is to identify, whenever possible, a comprehensive set of linguistic marks that would make these rules as unambiguous as possible in a certain application context.

Authoring tools and rule interface systems are useful for various kinds of operations including checking for duplicates and overlaps among large sets of rules. While some tools are available for sentence processing (e.g. (Sierra et al. 2008)), there is no such tool customized for discourse.

A number of investigations have been realized to identify linguistic marks on several discourse relations (Rosner et al 1992), (Redeker, 1990) (Marcu 1997), (Takechi et al. 2003) and (Stede 2012). These mostly establish general principles and methods to extract terms characterizing these relations.

In our approach to discourse analysis, rules are written by hand (i.e. rules do not result from automatic learning procedures from corpora). Although this is not the main trend nowadays, we feel this is the most reliable approach given the complexity and variability of discourse structures and the need to elaborate semantic representations. Let us briefly review the different steps involved in the rule production.

The first step, given a discourse function one wants to investigate, is to produce a clear definition of what it exactly represents and what its scope is, possibly in contrast with other functions. This is realized via a first corpus analysis where a number of realizations of this function over several domains are collected, analyzed and sorted by decreasing prototypicality order. This must be realized not by a single person but preferably by a few people, in a collaborative manner, and in connection with the literature, in order to reach the best consensus.

Then a larger corpus must be elaborated possibly using bootstrapping tools. Morpho-syntactic tagging contributes to identifying regularities and frequencies. From this corpus, a categorization of the different lexical resources which are needed must be elaborated. Then rules and lexical entries can be produced. Rules should be expressed at the right level of abstraction to account for a certain level of predictability and linguistic adequacy. This means avoiding low level rules (one rule per exceptional case) or too high level rules which would be difficult to constrain. In order to clearly identify text spans involved in a given discourse function, rules must be well-delimited, starting and ending by non-terminal or terminal symbols which are as specific of the construct as possible. Each rule should implement a particular form of a discourse function.

In general, the number of rules needed to describe a discourse relation (which form a cluster of rules) ranges from 5 to about 25 rules. In average, about 8 to 10 are really generic, while the others relate more restricted situations. This means that managing such a set of rules and evaluating them for a given function on a test corpus is feasible.

The next step is to order rules in the cluster, starting by the most constrained ones considering the processing strategy implemented in <TextCoop>. In general, the most constrained rules correspond to less frequent constructions than the generic ones, which could be viewed as the by-default ones. In this case, this means for the processing system going through a number of rules with little chances of success, involving useless computations. As an alternative, it is possible to start by generic rules if (1) they correspond to frequently encountered structures and (2) they start by typical symbols not present in the beginning of other rules. In this case, there is no ambiguity and backtracking will occur immediately. This is a compromise, frequently encountered in Logic Programming that needs to be evaluated by the rule author for each situation.

Overlap of new rules with already existing ones (in the same cluster or in other clusters) must be investigated since this will generate ambiguities. This is essentially a syntactic task that requires rule inspection. This task could certainly be automated in an authoring tool. If it turns out that ambiguities cannot be resolved, then preferences must be stated: a certain relation must be preferred to another one. Preferences can then be coded in the cascade, starting with the preferred rule clusters, then the recognition of competing rules can be excluded via constraints, as presented in the previous chapter (zone exclusion for example).

The last stage for rule writing is the development of selective binding rules and possibly correction rules for anomalous situations. Selective binding rules are relatively easy to produce since they are based on the binding of two already identified structures. These are essentially based on already produced html tags. Structure variability, long-distance relations or dislocations are automatically managed by the <TextCoop> engine, in a transparent way.

Finally, the rule writer must add the cluster name at the right place in the cascade and possibly state constraints as explained in Chapter 4.

Although there are important variations, the total amount of work for encoding from scratch a discourse relation of a standard complexity, including corpus collection, readings and testing should take a maximum of about one month full-time. This is a very reasonable amount of time considering e.g. the workload devoted to corpus annotation in the case of a machine learning approach.

We feel the quality of manual encoding is also better, in particular rule authors are aware of the potential weaknesses of their descriptions. Next, if a rule or a small set of rules are already available in an informal way with the need of minor revisions, then encoding this small set in Dislog is much faster: checking for needed lexical resources, writing the rules, checking overlaps and testing the system on a toy text should not take more than a day or two for a somewhat trained person. Our current environment contains about 280 rules describing 16 discourse structures associated with argumentation and explanation. These rules are essentially the core rules for the 16 discourse structures given in Chapter 2: it is clear that they can be used as a kernel for developing variants or more specific rules for these structures, or for structures that share some similarities. This should greatly facilitate the development of new rules for trained authors as well as for novices.

Coming back to an authoring tool, it is necessary at a certain stage to have a clear policy to develop the lexical architecture associated with the rule system. Redundancies (e.g. developing marks for each function even if functions share a lot of them) should be eliminated as much as possible via a higher level of lexical description. This would also help update, reusability and extensions.

Illustrations

To conclude this chapter, let us comment with some detail a few examples provided in the archive. The goal is to allow the reader to be able to write his own rules. The examples given in this section are explained in Chapter 2.

The Circumstance Function

This function analyses the circumstances under which an instruction must be carried out. In procedural documents it is in general expressed in a very simple way.

The main rule is the following:

```
forme(circ-eng,
E, S,
[expr(EXP,circ,E,E1),
gap([],[ponct,co],E1,E2,Saute1),
ponct(Ponct,co,E2,S)],
[],
['<circumstance>', EXP, Saute1, '</circumstance>', Ponct ]).
```

The three first arguments in that rule are the rule identifier, and the input output strings (E,S). Next comes the rule body, where an expression of type circ is first expected (a word that introduces a circumstance, as given in the lexical entries below). Then a gap will skip any kind of words until a punctuation mark is found. The next argument is empty ([]) since there is no reasoning involved at this level. The rule ends by a list where the original sentence is reproduced with XML marks inserted at a certain place, which can be decided freely. To reproduce the original sentence, variables that appear in the symbols are reused in this latter structure in an appropriate order. For example, EXP represents the expression, Saute1 what gap has skipped and Ponct is the punctuation symbol. In this last structure of the rule, an opening XML tag starts the expression, followed by EXP, Saute1 and then the closing XML tag and Ponct. It is possible to have the punctuation mark before the XML tag. In that case, the result is:

```
['<circumstance>', EXP, Saute1, Ponct, '</circumstance>']
```

Tags are given between quotes since they represent strings of characters. Note that if you wish to put the words of an input sentence in a different order, it is possible to insert the variables corresponding to words in a different order in this last argument, as shown above for the punctuation. Tags may also contain variables elaborated in the rule or in the reasoning part.

In the lexicon, in DCG format, typical marks expressing circumstance are for example the following:

```
expr([when],circ) --> [when].
expr([once],circ) --> [once].
expr([as,soon,as],circ) --> [as,soon,as].
expr([after],circ) --> [after].
expr([before],circ) --> [before].
expr([until],circ) --> [until].
expr([till],circ) --> [till].
expr([during],circ) --> [during].
expr([while],circ) --> [while].
```

In these lexical entries, the string of words corresponding to the mark appears in the first argument, the second argument contains the type of the mark, which is an arbitrary symbol (here circ). Since the type is in this case a unique constant, it is not represented as a list of features, but this last option is recommended if one wants uniform representations of lexical entries. Note that some of these marks are ambiguous and may also be used in other discourse functions. For example *while* may also be used to express contrasts.

A structure such as the following is then produced:

this will allow you to make adjustment for square < circumstance> once the plumbing is connected < /circumstance>

where "once" is the mark for the circumstance function.

The Illustration Function

Let us consider here two typical rules for the illustration function, among the 20 rules we have defined. These two rules allow the recognition of the satellite part, the term which is illustrated being much more difficult to recognize, as explained in Chapter 2.

```
% case 2a: recognizes: (for example : ....... )
forme(illus-eng,
 E, S,
[ponct(Ponct,po,E,E1),
ill_exempl(Ex,fe,E1,E2),
ponct(Ponct1,co,E2,E3),
gap([],[ponct,pf],E3,E4,Saute1),
ponct(Ponct2,pf,E4,S)],
[],
['<illustration>', Ponct, Ex, Ponct1, Saute1, Ponct2, '</illustration>']).

% case 2b: recognizes: ( ...... , for example )
forme(illus-eng,
E, S,
[ponct(Ponct,po,E,E1),
gap([],[ponct,co],E1,E2,Saute1),
ponct(Ponct1,co,E2,E3),
ill_exempl(Ex,fe,E3,E4),
ponct(Ponct2,pf,E4,S)],
[],
['<illustration>', Ponct, Saute1, Ponct1, Ex, Ponct2, '</illustration>']).
```

The first rule above (case 2a) deals with illustrations which are included between parentheses starting with a mark, e.g.:
(for example, ducks, geese and hens)
If we concentrate on the fourth argument, the structure to recognize, this argument starts by the recognition of a punctuation of type po (opening parenthesis). The second symbol is the illustration mark (lexical entry ill_exempl) which is here of type fe (standing for "for example" or equivalent marks), then follows a punctuation of type co, a gap (to skip the elements of the illustration itself), and the pattern ends by a punctuation mark of type closing parenthesis, noted pf.

The result is the concatenation of the original strings, in their reading order, preceded and followed by the appropriate XML marks. It is crucial to use different variable names for the different symbols which are used (several punctuations for example), as required in Prolog syntax.

The second rule above (case 2b) recognizes illustrations where the list of elements of the illustration appear right after the opening parenthesis, they are then followed by a comma and the mark "for example", or equivalent:

(ducks, geese and hens, for instance)

Lexical entries corresponding to these rules are, for example:

```
ponct(['.'],co) --> ['.'].
ponct([','],co) --> [','].
ponct([':'],co) --> [':'].
ponct([';'],co) --> [';'].
ponct(['parentouvr'],po) --> ['parentouvr'].
ponct(['parenthferm'],pf) --> ['parenthferm'].

ill_exempl([for,example],fe) --> [for,example].
ill_exempl([for,instance],fe) --> [for,instance].
```

These lexical entries have the same format as above. Note that parentouvre and parenthferm respectively refer to opening and closing parenthesis: since these symbols belong to the Prolog language, when processing a text, it is advised to replace any parenthesis by such a word to avoid any problem. When producing the output text, it is then possible to restore the original parenthesis.

As the reader may note it, the typing of marks is a delicate problem, it may also seem somewhat *ad hoc*. It is sometimes necessary to develop different kinds of typing for distinct discourse structures. In that case, this may involve duplicating lexical entries. Similarly, in the rules above, we have introduced a different identifier for the illustration marks (ill_exempl). The goal is to show that the rule author can choose the symbol identifiers he finds the most appropriate. This approach allows us to construct different modules of marks which are proper to each discourse structure. This may introduce some form of redundancy, but this greatly facilitates updates when they are local to a structure. It should also be noted that such marks are not so numerous, making the approach tractable.

The Reformulation Function

An implementation in Dislog of the reformulation function can be realized by the following rule:

```
% case 1: e.g.: in other words X ;
```

```
forme(restate-eng,
E, S,
[opt(ponct(Ponct,cor,E,E1)),
expr_reform(EXP,reform,E1,E2),
gap([],[ponct,cor],E2,E3,Saute1),
ponct(Ponct2,cor,E3,S)],
[],
[Ponct, '<restatement1>', EXP, Saute1, '</restatement>', Ponct2]).
```

The fourth argument of the above rule (the pattern to find in a sentence) starts by an optional punctuation: this punctuation is found when the reformulation is not at the beginning of a sentence:
A, in other words B
otherwise, if the reformulation starts a sentence the punctuation is not present. Then, follows an expression typical of a reformulation, such as: *in other words, said differently*, etc. The gap corresponds to the contents of the reformulation and the pattern ends by a punctuation mark.

Lexical entries are then the following :

```
expr_reform([in,other,words], reform) --> [in,other,words].
expr_reform([to,put,it,another,way], reform)
                                        --> [to,put,it,another,way].
expr_reform([that,is,to,say], reform) --> [that,is,to,say].
expr_reform([put,differently], reform) --> [put,differently].
expr_reform([said,differently], reform) --> [said,differently].
expr_reform([otherwise,stated], reform) --> [otherwise,stated].
expr_reform([ie],_) --> [ie].
```

and:

```
ponct([','],cor) --> [','].
ponct([';'],cor) --> [';'].
```

Recognizing Instructions

Instructions in procedures are either in the infinitive or imperative form. This latter form is not different from the infinitive form in English. Finite forms are very infrequent and not recommended, as explained in Chapter 3. These are usually found in large public procedures such as video game solutions or simple computer manuals.

Besides this tense constraint, the main verb of an instruction must be an action verb. Action verbs form a very large set of verbs, more than

10 000 in English. However, for a given application this is much more restricted: from 300 to 700 for large public applications (cooking, DIY, gardening, etc.) and in general less than 150 for industrial domains. It is therefore quite simple to define this set of verbs and to control its usage in industrial documents. However, in English, there are many ambiguities between nouns and verbs (e.g. *iron* designates both an object and the typical use of this object: ironing; same for *fish, water*, etc.). If there is a risk of ambiguity, then it is necessary to develop a more elaborated grammar and parser. This problem does not occur in languages with a rich flexion system such as French or Spanish, where ambiguities are less frequent.

A rule that recognizes an instruction with an action verb in the infinitive form can be written as follows:

```
forme(instr-eng,
E, S,
[mdeb(MDEB,_,E,E1),
gap(neg, [verb,[action,inf]], E1,E2,Saute1),
verb(V,[action,inf],E2,E3),
gap([], [mfin,pt], E3,E4,Saute2),
 mfin(MFIN,pt,E4,S)],
[],
[ MDEB,'<instruction>' , Saute1, '<verb type=action> ',
                    V, '</verb>', Saute2,' </instruction>', MFIN ]).
```

In the pattern described by this rule (third argument), the first symbol, mdeb, recognizes the beginning of an instruction which can be e.g. the beginning of a sentence or of an enumeration, characterized by various kinds of typographic marks. Then a gap is introduced in order to skip words till an action verb in the infinitive form is found. The gap also requires that no negation is skipped before the verb is found: this constraint ensures that the sentence is not in the negative form, because it would then be interpreted as a warning (e.g. *do not throw the acid in the sewer*). If we want the verb to start the instruction without any other term before, this first gap must be deleted. The next symbol is the verb, constrained to be an action verb in the infinitive. Then follows a gap that skips the remainder of the utterance till an ending mark (mfin) is found.

In this rule there is no reasoning element. The rule ends by the reconstruction of the utterance that has been read with the introduction of XML marks. The <instruction> tag is inserted after the "beginning of utterance mark" and before the "end of utterance mark". This is a choice a priori which can be changed at will. For illustrative purposes, we have included tags that delimit the main verb of the instruction. Furthermore, the opening XML verb tag receives an attribute. Note that the constant "action" in that attribute could be inherited from the main verb via a variable.

The example given above is typical of instructions. Obviously there are many variants depending on the domain and the authoring recommendations. For example the actor could be mentioned in cases where several participants are involved. In that case, the verb is probably finite.

Conclusion

In this chapter, the use of Dislog and <TextCoop> has been presented. Concrete and simple situations have been developed so that the reader can start using the system with his own descriptions. Dislog can be used in a number of applications besides discourse analysis, where its formalism is appropriate. For example, Dislog has been used in a variety of applications, such as argument mining and opinion analysis.

From the four implementation samples developed in this chapter, the reader can see that most of the rules are relatively simple to write and that they are based on simple sets of marks, including punctuation. It is however clear that, to develop a real-size application, it is necessary to define a precise linguistic architecture for the different types of data, in particular lexical resources, and to manage potential overlaps between rule systems. For a given discourse function, it may also be useful to define priorities among rules to avoid conflicts and to improve efficiency. The rules presented in this chapter have been defined informally from a manual corpus analysis. We believe this is an efficient and linguistically adequate way to proceed. However, rules can also be produced from semi-supervised learning algorithms, where non-terminal and preterminal symbols emerge from this analysis.

In Chapter 6, we will see in more detail the syntax of requirement structures, which is another type of structure frequently found in technical documents. Requirements also use discourse functions proper to explanation.

CHAPTER SIX

AN ANALYSIS OF THE DISCOURSE STRUCTURE OF REQUIREMENTS

JUYEON KANG AND PATRICK SAINT-DIZIER

Introduction

In this chapter, we investigate in more depth the linguistic structure of requirements. The aim is to show how to improve requirement authoring and the overall coherence, cohesion and organization of requirement documents. This work will then allow accurate requirement extraction processes from texts (this is called requirement mining).

Design and software requirements must be unambiguous, short, relevant and easy to understand by professionals. The form and contents of safety requirements must be carefully checked since they may be as complex as procedures. Requirements must leave as little space as possible for personal interpretations. The different types of requirements and their main functions are presented in depth in e.g. (Hull et al. 2011), (Sage et al. 2009), (Grady 2006), (Pohl, 2010), and (Nuseibeh et al. 2000). A lot of work has been devoted to requirement engineering (indexing, traceability, organization), via systems such as e.g. Doors and its extensions (e.g. Reqtify, QuaARS). However, although they are written in natural language, very little attention has been devoted to the linguistic dimensions of requirements, besides a few works such as (Gnesi et al. 2005). Requirements are sometimes called business rules (developed in SBVR, where a few authoring principles are outlined). However, business rules have a somewhat wider scope, in connection with the domain ontology. Business rules are not developed in this chapter.

In this chapter, we first introduce requirements, their types and their functions. Then, we present the form documents containing requirements have in the industry. Next, we present two approaches to requirement authoring: based on the use of predefined templates called boilerplates and based on a posteriori controls, following the guidelines given in Chapter 3 of this book and in the Lelie project presented in Chapter 7. Finally, we investigate the discourse structure of requirements and define a number of rules that complement those given in Chapter 2 for procedures. Rules are written in Dislog. An evaluation of these rules used in the context of requirement mining is given that concludes this chapter.

In 1998, the IEEE-STD association defined requirements in a very general way as follows:

> *A requirement is a statement that identifies a product or process operational, functional, or design characteristic or constraint which is unambiguous, testable or measurable, and necessary for product or process acceptability (by consumers or internal quality assurance guidelines).*

This general definition is then somewhat elaborated by the IEEE with the three following points, a requirement states:

-a condition or capability needed by a user to solve a problem or achieve an objective,

-a condition or capability that must be met or possessed by a system or system component to satisfy a contract, standard, specification, or other formal document,

-a documented representation of a condition or capability of the two items above.

These definitions give a general framework for requirements, the second item being probably the most crucial.

Several types of requirements have been identified in the literature. They often have very different language realizations. The main types of requirements identified are described below, see also (Hull et al. 2011), (Sage et al. 2009), (Pohl, 2010). ***Project requirements*** define how the work at stake will be managed. These include the budget, the communication management, the resource management, the quality assurance, the risk management, and the scope management. Project requirements focus on the *who, when, where,* and *how* something gets done. They are generally documented in the Project Management Plan. ***Product requirements*** include high level features, specifications or capabilities that the business team has committed to deliver to a customer. Product requirements do not specify how the features or the capabilities of the product will be designed or realized. This is specified at a lower level. Product requirements include specification documents where the properties of a product are described prior to its realization. Specification documents often have a contractual dimension.

Functional requirements describe what the system does, what it must resolve or avoid. They include any requirement that outlines a specific way a product function or component must perform. These requirements are more specific than product requirements. However, they do not explain how they can be realized. Finally, ***Non-functional requirements*** develop elements such as technical solutions, the number of people who could use the product, where the product will be located, the types of transactions which can be processed, and the types of technology interactions. Non-functional requirements develop measurable constraints for functional requirements. A non-functional requirement may for example specify the amount of time it takes for a user with a given skill to realize a given action.

Requirements associated with a given product or activity are produced by different participants, often with different profiles. For example, stakeholders are at the initiative of requirements that describe the product they expect. Then, engineers, safety staff, regulation experts and technicians may produce more specialized requirements, for example: quality, tracing, modeling or testing requirements (Hull et al. 2011). These documents may then undergo several levels of validation and update. The requirement specifications and life cycles are often complex. This explains why it is necessary to control the writing quality of requirements, their contents and their homogeneity.

Requirements address a system as a whole and then its components and subsystems. Each component or subsystem may have its own requirements, possibly contradictory with those of the main system. Even for a small, limited product, it is frequent to have several thousand requirements, hierarchically organized.

Requirement specification is now becoming a major activity in the industry. The goal is to specify product properties or processes in a more rigorous, modular, abstract and manageable way. Requirements may be proper to a company, an activity or a country. In this latter case, it may be a regulation.

We now observe requirements in areas as diverse as product or software design, finance, communication, staff management and security and safety. These requirements have very different language forms. Software design are in general very concise and go to the point. At the other extreme, safety requirements can be very long, describing all the precautions to take in a given circumstance. They often resemble procedures: they start with a context (e.g. *manipulating acid*) and then develop the actions to undertake: *wear gloves, glasses*, etc.

To conclude this introduction, here are a few short illustrations:

-(1) Login: Each login and each role change MUST be protected via authentication process. Motivation: Special functions or administrative tasks are only possible based on a role change. Misuse of a user account with too many authorizations is sharply reduced.

-(2) A password MUST be at least 8 characters long. PINs can be shorter for special requirements and MUST be at least four characters in length. Motivation: A minimum length of 8 characters plus the use of a large range of characters offers sufficient protection against brute force attacks.

-(3) The equipment must be tested and compliant with the following requirements of the main environmental European Standards:
climatic: ETSI EN 300 019 (the corresponding temperature class must be clearly given) and ETSI EN 300 119-5
mechanic: ETSI EN 300 119-1 to -4
acoustic: ETS 300-753 (table 1)
chemical: ETSI EN 300 019-2-3, specification T3.1
transportation: ETSI EN 300 019-2-2, specification T 2.3

-(4) Where an ECP exists on a road which is to be improved or will be subjected to major maintenance, the Design Organisation, in conjunction with the Overseeing Organisation, must discuss with the relevant Emergency Services, the need for the ECP to be retained.

-(5) BOMB THREAT. In case of a bomb threat:
a) Any person receiving a telephone threat should try to keep the caller on the line and if possible transfer the Area Manager. Remain calm, notify your supervisor and await instructions.
a) If you are unable to transfer the call, obtain as much relevant information as possible and notify the Area Manager by messenger. Try to question the caller so you can fill out the 'Bomb Threat Report Form'. After the caller hangs up, notify the Division Manager, then contact 911 and ask for instructions. Then contact Maintenance and the Governor's office.
c) The Division Manager will call the police (911) for instructions.
c1. If the Division Manager is not available call 911 and wait for instructions.
c2. Pull EMERGENCY EVACUATION ALARM. Follow evacuation procedures.

d) The person who received the bomb threat will report directly to the police station.

The first two examples are relatively short statements typical of software design. They include a kind of explanation: the motivations for such a constraint, so that the requirement is clearly understood and accepted by the designer. The third example is related to the application of a regulation with the list of the different norms to consider. The fourth one is related to management and work organization. The last one is a typical (short) safety requirement implemented in a precise company (general safety requirements must often be customized to local environments). The requirement starts by a title and the context (*bomb threat*) and then it is followed by a structured list of instructions which are designed to be short and easy to understand by all the staff of that company.

Requirement Writing and Control

Requirement production is often a complex process that involves various actors and hierarchy levels. The different types of actors have been advocated above. It is frequent, in particular for safety requirements or generic requirements, that they undergo several steps of specification and then customization to precise environments. For example, a government can produce general regulations about the use of chemical products. Then, public or private institutions may develop a more specialized description of these regulations for a given type or class of chemical product, going into more details, possibly interpreting the government regulations. Then, at the end of this process, safety engineers adapt theses descriptions to their company and environment, product by product, activity by activity, possibly also building by building (e.g. fire alarm and related actions may differ from one building to another). Through all these steps, writing and coherence problems may easily arise.

Requirements must follow authoring principles and recommendations. Recommendations are in general quite close to those elaborated for procedural texts. A few norms have been produced and international standards have recently emerged. Let us note in particular: (1) IEEE Standard 830- Requirement Specification: "Content and qualities of a good software requirement specification" and (2) IEEE Standard 1233, "Guide for developing System Requirements Specifications".

In Chapter 3, we present some general principles for requirement elicitation and writing, following (Buddenberg 2010). There are a few form differences between requirements and procedures: for example modals are central to requirements (the use of *must, shall*), negation is also frequent. Let us now review two of the main approaches to requirement authoring: boilerplates and *a posteriori* control.

Boilerplates: a Template-Based Approach

The boilerplate approach was developed for writing requirements in software and product design. These requirements are often very short sentences which follow very strict and regular formats. Boilerplates is a technique that uses simple predefined language templates based on concepts and relations to guide and control requirement descriptions. These templates may be combined to form larger structures. Requirement authors must follow these templates. Boilerplates define the language of requirements. The RAT-RQA approach developed by the Reuse-company is a typical example. Defining such a language is not straightforward for complex requirements such as safety requirements, financial and management requirements.

The language introduced by boilerplates allows to write simple propositions as well as more specialized components which are treated as adjuncts, such as capability of a system, capacity (maximize, exceed), rapidity, mode, sustainability, timelines, operational constraints and exceptions. Repositories of boilerplates have been defined by companies or research groups, these may be generic or activity dependent. An average size repository has about 60 boilerplates. Larger repositories are more difficult to manage. These are not in general publicly available.

The examples below illustrate the constructions proposed by boilerplates. Terms in bold between < > are concepts which must receive a language expression possibly subject to restrictions:

General purpose boilerplates:

-The **<SYSTEM>** shall be able to **<capability>**.

The washing machine *shall be able to* wash the dirty clothes.

-The **<SYSTEM>** shall be able to **<action> <entity>**.

The ACC system *shall be able to* determine the speed of the eco-vehicle.

The use of the modal *shall* in the frames is typical of requirements. In the above examples, the concept *action* is realized as a verb, the concept *entity* as a direct object and the concept *capability* as a verb phrase. The syntactic structures associated with each of these concepts are relatively well identified. The different terms which are used such as e.g. *entities* can be checked by reference to the domain ontology and terminology.

Boilerplates can then be defined in terms of a combination of specialized constructions inserted into general purpose ones. They may have various levels of granularity. In the examples below, modals, prepositions and quantifiers are imposed:

-The **<SYSTEM>** shall **<function>** **<object>** every **<performance>** **<units>**.

The coffee machine *shall* produce a hot drink *every* 10 seconds.

-The **<system>** shall **<function>** not less than **<quantity>** **<object>** while **<operational conditions>**.

The communications system *shall* sustain telephone contact *with not less than* 10 callers *while* in the absence of external power.

-The **<SYSTEM>** shall display status messages in **<circumstance>**.

The Background Task Manager *shall display status messages in* a designated area of the user interface at intervals of 60 plus or minus 10 seconds.

-The < **SYSTEM** > shall be able to **<function>** **<object>** composed of not less than **<performance>** **<units>** with **<external entity>**.

-The < **SYSTEM** > shall be able to **<function>** **<object>** of type **<qualification>** within **<performance>** **<units>**.

-While **<operational condition>** the **<stakeholder>** shall **<capability>**.

While activated *the* driver *shall* be able to override engine power control of the ACC-system.

-The **<stakeholder>** shall not be placed in breach of **<applicable law>**.

The ambulance driver *shall not be placed in breach of* national road regulations.

As the reader may note it, the user of such a concept-based system needs some familiarity with these concepts to be able to use boilerplates correctly. Some types are relatively vague, allowing large language variations, while others are very constrained. These latter require some training and documentation for the novice technical writer. Additional tools can be defined to help writing each concept.

The use of boilerplates has some advantages when producing large sets of short requirements in the sense that predefined templates guide the author, limiting the revisions needed at the form level. Revisions are still required at the contents level because a number of types remain abstract and somewhat vague (*performance, operational conditions, capability*, etc.). It is however an attempt to standardize the requirement sublanguage, at least from a lexical and syntactic point of view. Due to the rigid character of boilerplates, a difficulty may arise when authors embed too many boilerplates: instead of being clear the formulation risk to be very complex and obscure.

Using predefined attributes makes it to easier to write requirements for authors, in particular those with limited experience. Authors can select the most appropriate templates and instantiate concepts such as *capability, condition*. However, this language must not evolve so much, otherwise large revisions of already produced requirements will need to be updated. New templates can be added, but it is not possible to remove existing ones or to transform their structure.

Limitations of boilerplates are related to the low level of freedom that is offered to writers. The expressive power of boilerplates must be tuned to the needs of a given activity. Furthermore, authors which do not have a good command of the concepts and of what they cover will have a lot of difficulties to use boilerplates, this is obviously the case of stakeholders. Therefore, boilerplates may be used essentially for technical requirements.

An *a posteriori* Control of the Language Quality of Requirements

A different approach allows requirement authors to produce their documents rather freely and to offer them a tool to control their production *a posteriori*, upon demand. This is obviously a much less constraining view that leaves more freedom and flexibility to the author. This approach is well-adapted for experienced authors and for domains or areas where requirements are complex, for example security requirements or regulations which may be several pages long. In that case, boilerplates are not appropriate. This is the approach chosen in the Lelie project presented in Chapter 7.

Authors can ask for controls on the form (lexicon, business terms, grammar, style, etc.) and on the contents when they feel they have written something which is stable. Controls can be made on sentences, paragraphs, sections or on the whole document. Controls can also be parameterized to the type of structures to check, how and when. Author profiles can be introduced, to take into account e.g. their writing skills, writing habits, or the nature of the control and the rights they have on the document. This approach, similarly to boilerplates, can also be used as a tutoring system for beginners.

In Chapter 3, we have presented some features requirements must follow to be as unambiguous and easy to use as possible. We develop below additional general purpose considerations on the way requirement authors could proceed when they write documents. Some elements emerged from (Buddenberg 2011). These considerations complement those developed in Chapter 3, they are however more difficult to implement in a system since they deal with general methodological aspects.

The first advice is to make sure a requirement statement is ***sufficiently well defined***. To see if a requirement statement is sufficiently well defined, it must be read from the developer's perspective. Mentally add the phrase, "*call me when you're done*" to the end of the requirement and see if that makes you nervous. In other words, would you need additional clarification from the requirement author to understand the requirement well enough to design and implement it? If so, this requirement should be further elaborated.

Next, it is crucial to find the ***right level of granularity***. It is important to avoid long narrative paragraphs that contain several requirements or multiple views on a requirement. A helpful granularity guideline is to write individually testable requirements. A strategy is to think of a small number of related tests to verify the correct implementation of a requirement. If so, it is probably written at the right level of detail. If many different kinds of tests are envisioned, perhaps several requirements have been lumped together and should be separated.

Then it is important to watch out for ***multiple requirements that have been aggregated*** into a single statement. Conjunctions like "and" and "or" in a requirement suggest that several requirements have been combined. Avoid to use "and/or" in a requirement statement.

Then authors should write requirements at a ***consistent level of detail*** throughout the whole document. For example, "*a valid color code shall be R for red*" and "*the best color code for green is a small tree*" do not have a consistent form.

Finally, authors should avoid ***stating requirements redundantly*** in the requirement document. While including the same requirement in multiple places may make the document easier to read, it also makes maintenance of the document more difficult. The multiple instances of a given requirement all have to be updated at the same time: an inconsistency can creep into the document easily.

The Discourse Structure of Requirement Documents

In this section we develop the structure of requirement documents. Requirements may come in isolation, as structured lists, or they can be embedded into larger documents. We first address the organization of requirements in larger documents, and then focus on the internal structure of requirements. We show that requirements often have a complex discourse structure.

Our analysis of requirements is based on a corpus of requirements coming from 7 companies, kept anonymous at their request. Documents are in French or English. Our corpus contains about 500 pages extracted from 27 documents. These 27 documents are composed of 15 French and 12 English documents. The main features considered to validate our corpus are the following:

-requirements correspond to various professional activities: product design, management, finance, and safety,

-requirements correspond to different conceptual levels: functional, realization, management, etc.

-requirements follow various kinds of business style and format guidelines,

-requirements come from various industrial areas: finance, telecommunications, transportation, energy, computer science, and chemistry.

Diversity of forms and contents in this corpus allows us to capture the main linguistic features of requirements. We focus here on the linguistic and discursive structures of requirements, which parallel their logical structure. The logical structure has been widely addressed in the literature, as in e.g. (Hull et al. 2011), (Sage et al. 2009), (Grady 2006), (Pohl, 2010).

Considering the complexity of the discourse structures associated with requirements, we carried out a manual analysis of the corpus. We proceeded by generalizing over closely related language cues identified from sets of examples, as introduced in (Marcu 1997), (Takechi et al 2003), (Saito 2006) and (Bourse et al. 2011) for procedural texts. Rules describing the structure of requirements are then manually elaborated. Using automatic acquisition methods would have required the annotation of very large sets of documents, which are difficult to obtain.

In general, in most types of specifications, requirements are organized by purpose or theme. Their organization follows principles given in e.g. (Rossner et al. 1992). The structure of these specifications is highly hierarchical and very modular, often following authoring and organization principles proper to a company or to an organization. Requirements may be associated with formulae, diagrams or pictures. This will not be investigated here.

The higher level of requirement documents often starts with general considerations such as purpose, scope, or context. Then follow definitions, examples, scenarios or schemas. Next, a series of sections address the different facets of the problem at stake by means of sets of requirements. Each section may include general purpose elements followed by the relevant requirements. Requirements can just be listed in an appropriate order or be preceded by comments. Each requirement can include e.g. conditions or warnings and forms of explanation such as justifications, reformulations or illustrations.

One of the challenges of discourse analysis is to be able to capture all the "adjuncts" that characterize a requirement and give their scope, purpose, limitations, priority and semantics. This is an important difficulty in requirement mining. This is illustrated below. Due to the complexity of the underlying semantics of discourse structures, this is a long-term research topic.

The structure of Requirement Kernels

A requirement is often composed of a main part, called its kernel, and additional elements such as conditions, goals or purposes, illustrations, and various constraints. Let us first address the structure of requirement kernels. By kernel, we mean the main clause of the requirement. As introduced in the section dedicated to boilerplates, requirements have quite a strict structure. We review below the main structures found in our corpus. These are presented under the form of Dislog rules, in an external, readable format, as in Chapter 2 where explanation structures are developed.

While most documents share a large number of similarities in requirement expression, there is also quite a large diversity of structures which are only found in a subset of them. We categorized 20 prototypical structures for English which have different linguistic structures. These can be summarized, modulo lexical parameters, by the following eight rules.

In these rules, the symbols bos (beginning of structure) and eos (end of structure) are characterized by a punctuation, a connector, or simply the beginning or the end of a sentence or of an enumeration. Html marks can also be considered as starters or ending marks. These marks are crucial: they define the boundaries of requirements, whereas lexical marks allow the identification of requirements. Gaps allow the system to skip finite sets of words of no present interest (see Chapter 4).

The rules we have defined are the following:

(1) Lexically induced requirements: in this case, the main verb of the clause is *to require* or a closely related verb. The verb is marked with a requiretype constraint, which is a lexical constraint:

requirement → bos, gap, verb(requiretype), gap, eos.

Company X requires equipment that comply with relevant environment standards (EMC, safety, resistibility, powering, air conditioning, sustainable growth, acoustic, etc.).

(2) Requirements composed of a modal applied to an action verb: a large number of requirements are characterized by the use of a modal (in general *must* or *shall*) applied to an action verb in the infinitive. This construction has a strong injunctive orientation. The lexical type action denotes verbs which describe concrete actions. This excludes a priori (but this depends on the context) state verbs, psychological verbs and some epistemic verbs (*know, deduce,* etc.). Adverb phrases are optional, they often introduce aspectual or manner considerations:

requirement → bos, gap, modal, {advP}, verb(action, infinitive), gap, eos.

The solution, software or equipment shall support clocks synchronization with an agreed accurate time source.

(3) Requirement composed of a modal, the auxiliary *be* and an action verb used as a past participle:

requirement → bos, gap, modal, aux(be), {advP}, verb(action, past-participle), gap, eos.

Where new safety barriers are required and gaps of 50 m or less arise between two separate safety barrier installations, where practicable, the gap must be closed and the safety barrier made continuous.

(4) A special case, with the same structure as in (3), are requirements which use an expression of type "conformity" instead of an action verb, as, e.g. *to be compliant with, to comply with.* The auxiliary *be* may be included in this expression. The modal must be present to implement the injunctive character of the expression:

requirement → bos, gap, modal, {advP}, expr(conform), gap, eos.

All safety barriers must be compliant with the Test Acceptance Criteria.

(5) A number of requirements include comparative or superlative forms or the expression of a minimal or maximal quantity or amount of an entity or of a resource. The modal is present and the main verb is the auxiliary *have*, which plays here the role of a light verb. In the rule below, expr(quantity) calls a local grammar that

recognizes various forms of expressions of quantity that include a constraint (maximal, minimal, superlative, comparative). These constraints are often realized by means of specific lexical items such as *at least one, a maximum of, not more than*, etc.

requirement → bos, gap, modal, have, expr(quantity), gap, eos

Physical entities must have at least one Ethernet interface per zone it is connected to (front, back, administrative)

The rule with the comparative form with the auxiliary *be* writes as follows. The symbol comparative_form is a call to a local grammar that describes the structure of comparative forms (*equal to, greater than*, etc.)

requirement → bos, gap, modal, aux(be), comparative_form, gap, eos.

For all other roads, the Containment Level at the ECP/MCP shall be equal to or greater than that of the adjacent safety barrier e.g. if the safety barrier is N2, then the ECP/MCP must also have a minimum N2 Containment Level.

(6) Requirements expressing a property to be satisfied. This class of requirements is more difficult to characterize since properties may be written in a large number of ways. Marks can be adjectives, or more complex business terms. In the rule below, the property is skipped, while the construction "*must be*" is kept since it is typical of requirements. However, this rule is not totally satisfactory as it stands since it may over-generates incorrect structures.

requirement → bos, gap, modal, aux(be), gap, eos.

For terminals that face oncoming traffic, e.g. those at both ends of a VRS on a two-way single Carriageway road, the minimum Performance Class must be P4.

(7) When a document is a list of requirements without any other form of text, it is frequent that the modal *must* is omitted because there is no need to have specific marks for requirements. The modal is simply underlying. In that case, the rule is similar to an instruction with an action verb in the infinitive:

requirement → bos, verb(action, infinitive), gap, eos.

Leave a 1 / 8 - inch gap between the panels.

These rules require lexical resources, in particular: modals, auxiliaries, action verbs, and adjectives referring to performance, completion, necessity or conformity. The open lexical categories can be constructed from corpus inspection and the addition of closely related terms. In general the vocabulary which is used in technical texts is not very large, except for business terms, which are often defined in a terminology.

These rules have been implemented in Dislog and run on the <TextCoop> platform. The system produces annotations of the following form (verbs are also tagged with their morphology: pp = past participle, inf = infinitive):

<requirement> running services must be <verb type = "pp"> restricted </verb> to the strict minimum </requirement>

<requirement> equipments must < verb type = "inf"> provide < /verb> acl filtering </requirement>

<requirement> physical entities must have at least one Ethernet interface per zone it is connected to (front, back, administrative) </requirement>

<requirement> every administrative access must be initiated from a rebound server using a set of predetermined tools </requirement>

<requirement> for shared services, a shared information system interface enabler is <verb type = “pp"> required </verb> to route real time charging messages to local systems </requirement>

The above rules can be used in a number of applications. We have evaluated their use and accuracy in the requirement mining framework (see e.g. Sampaio et al. 2005). The task was, given a set of texts, to evaluate how accurate these rules are to identify requirements.

The corpus considered for evaluation has the following characteristics:

File ID	French	English
Doc1	Texts extracted from 15 documents used as the development corpus *28 pages, 8,147 words*	Texts extracted from 12 documents used as the development corpus *23 pages, 7,479 words*
Doc2	Texts randomly selected from corpora concerning biomedical engineering and telecommunication *33 pages, 9,511 words*	Texts randomly selected from corpora concerning e-finance, telecommunication and mechanical handling *41 pages, 14,759 words*
Total	*61 pages,17,658 words*	*64 pages, 22,238 words*

Table 6-1 Requirement analysis: the evaluation corpus

The file doc1 allows us to check if the system works correctly and doc2 allows us to evaluate the accuracy of the system on a different set of documents. This constitutes an indicative evaluation of the performances of the rules.

Both doc1 and doc2 have been manually annotated and the results reported below are based on a comparison between the manually annotated texts and the results produced by the rules implemented on the <TextCoop> platform. Results are the following:

situations	French		English	
	Doc1	Doc2	Doc1	Doc2
Manually Annotated requirements	108	35	174	45
Structures identified as requirements by the system	103	30	175	40
Erroneously tagged structures	1	0	1	6
Requirements not recognized	6	5	0	11
Accuracy (total errors/ total manually tagged)	94%	86%	99%	76%

Table 6-2 Accuracy of requirement mining

Summing up all these results, we obtain a precision of 99% for French and 96% for English and a recall of 92% for French and 95% for English. Results are obviously better for doc1 than doc2 since doc1 is part of the development corpus.

These results are really good. This is for a large part due to the fact that requirements follow very strict authoring guidelines. Their recognition is therefore a rather easy task with a modest number of rules compared to discourse analysis in general.

At the moment, there are, surprisingly, very few systems that use natural language processing techniques to analyze the structure of requirements with the goal to contribute to their improvement (authoring, traceability, consistency checking, clustering, etc.). Let us note the system QuaARS (Gnesi et al. 2005) and, to a lesser extent, Lexior.

Complex Requirements Analysis

Requirement kernels are often associated with various discourse structures. The structures developed in Chapter 2 for explanation are all applicable to requirements. It is of particular interest to analyze the discourse structures which are adjuncts to requirement kernels: conditions, goals, purpose, circumstance, illustration, restatement, etc. These structures are within the scope of a requirement or a group of requirements. In this latter case this is clearly marked in the syntax or via typographic indications. Explanations may therefore have scope over conjunctions of requirements.

In the implementation, the principle is to first analyze discourse structures. Then requirements are processed. The integration of discourse structures into a requirement scope is realized by means of one or more selective binding rules. The rule application order must be specified in the cascade of automata, as specified in Chapter 4.

Our implementation enables the recognition of a variety of complex requirements such as:

<requirement>
< condition> if required by the distributor< /condition> ,
we must be able to bill all usages on a single wallet and supervised some postpaid account </requirement> .

<requirement>
the tenderer shall <verb type = "inf"> detail </verb> the average duration for the different phase of the development of a new release of its product release definition , design , implementation , unit test , end
<purpose> in order to end tests. </purpose> </requirement>.

<requirement>
for each of the network elements included in its solution, the tenderer shall <verb type = "inf "> describe </verb> which hardware components
<illustration> ie racks, chassis, servers, blades, processing units, i/o cards, mother cards, daughter cards etc </illustration>
of its overall platform are redundant < /requirement>.

<requirement>
<condition> if geo redundancy is feasible </condition> ,
the tenderer will indicate which requirements ,

<illustration> such as minimum link throughput , maximum latency , and maximum distance between sites </illustration>,
have to be met in order to achieve geographical stateful redundancy </requirement>.

<requirement>
the performance figures provided here should be measured
<circumstance> when the full functional capabilities of the platform are activated </circumstance> </requirement>.

<requirement>
the bidder must <verb type = "inf "> identify </verb> the information being held allowing the operator
<purpose> to determine the sensitivity of the information </purpose>
and mandate the level of protection required </requirement>.

<requirement>
in case the solution, software or equipment is connected to an ip network
<illustration> (being public, private, administration or uncontrolled) </illustration>,
connectivity,
<circumstance> when needed </circumstance> ,
shall < verb type = "inf "> support < /verb> ciphered transport protocols
< illustration> such as , but not limited to , ipsec , tls / ssl , ssh , etc </illustration> </requirement>.

<requirement>
solution , software or equipment must be able to be adequately managed and controlled,
<goal> in order to be protected from threats </goal> , and
<purpose> to maintain security for the systems and applications using the network <illustration> including information in transit </illustration>
</purpose>, </requirement>.

Besides the use of the modals *shall* or *must*, the reader can observe the use of other modals: e.g. *should* and *will* which have a lower injunctive or persuasion force. This is of interest to implicitly give priorities to requirements. Company guideline often specify the modals which are allowed and how they must be interpreted.

Conclusion

In this chapter, we have presented several features of requirements: (1) their purpose and the different forms they can have, and (2) authoring recommendations so that requirements can be understood straightforwardly. Two main trends govern the way requirements can be produced: the boilerplate approach, based on the use of predefined templates, and an *a posteriori* control of the quality of the language. We have outlined the advantages and limitations of each of these approaches. The second approach has been adopted in the LELIE project which is presented in Chapter 7.

Then, we developed the structure of requirement kernels. We also presented some simple elements and an evaluation for requirement mining based on the requirement analysis we have developed. Requirements have relatively rigid forms. This entails that their recognition is a relatively feasible task with a good accuracy.

CHAPTER SEVEN

THE LELIE PROJECT: RISK ANALYSIS AND PREVENTION FROM TECHNICAL DOCUMENTS

PATRICK SAINT-DIZIER

Introduction

In the last chapter of this book, some features of the LELIE project are introduced. LELIE is a project funded by the French *Agence Nationale de la Recherche* (ANR). The goal of this project is to analyze and prevent risks of various kinds from an accurate analysis of technical texts from the point of view of their form and their contents. This project is therefore a kind of concrete illustration and implementation of several principles and methods presented in this book.

The LELIE project develops an analysis, a linguistic model and then a piece of software based on language processing and artificial intelligence that detects and analyses potential risks of different kinds (in relation with health and ecology, but also social and financial risks) in technical documents. The project concentrates on procedural documents (Chapter 2 and 3) and on requirements (Chapter 6) which are the main types of technical documents used in companies which can raise safety problems.

Given a set of procedures over a certain domain produced by a company, and given some domain knowledge (characterized e.g. by its ontology, terminology, and lexical data), the goal is to process these procedures and to annotate them wherever potential risks are identified. Authors are then invited to revise these documents.

Similarly, requirements, in particular those related to safety (e.g. public regulations), often exhibit complex linguistic structures such as several embedded conditions, negation, pronouns, etc., which make their understanding and use difficult, especially in emergency situations. As developed in Chapter 1, procedures as well as safety requirements are dedicated to action: little space should be left to hesitations or to personal interpretations. Therefore controlling the form of these documents, in addition to their contents, is an important issue and challenge.

Risk analysis and prevention in LELIE are based on three levels of analysis, each of them potentially leading to errors. This project has the following three main objectives:

-***The detection of inappropriate ways of writing texts***, as, for example: use of complex expressions, implicit elements, complex references, scoping situations difficult to interpret (e.g. for negation, connectors, conditionals), inappropriate uses of business terms and inadequate granularity levels for instructions, as developed in Chapter 3.

-***The detection of domain dependent incoherencies*** in procedures: detection of unusual ways of realizing an action (e.g. unusual instrument, equipment, product, unusual value such as temperature, voltage, length of treatment, etc.). This unusual character is evaluated w.r.t. similar actions related to the same activity in other procedures or w.r.t. to data extracted from technical documents. This may require the use of a domain knowledge base.

-***The confrontation of safety requirements with procedures*** to check if the relevant safety constraints are correctly implemented in procedures (comprehensively and at the right place). Only simple safety requirements, such as individual protections or work in cold, noisy or elevated areas, have been considered in this project due to the conceptual complexity of safety requirements in general.

The LELIE project is obviously very vast. We mainly concentrate in this chapter on the first task which is central to this book: the detection of inappropriate ways of authoring procedures and requirements. The two other levels are more oriented towards artificial intelligence and knowledge representation processes and models, they require less discourse processing than this first level.

This chapter is partly elaborated from (Barcellini et al. 2012). Note that procedures and safety requirements share some linguistic and conceptual characteristics since they are forms of operational style, but with their own specificities. Requirements are of two types: prevention requirements (how to avoid risks) and emergency ones (what to do when a problem occurs). These two types of documents are treated in the same way in this project. However, only the first type can be checked in procedures in relation with the Objective 3 above.

The documents we consider in this project range from short emergency notices to large procedures which may be more than 100 pages long.

These large documents often follow specific authoring guidelines which must also be taken into account and checked, similarly to grammatical and general style constraints.

Risk management and prevention are now a major issue. This issue is developed at several levels, in particular via probabilistic analysis of risks in complex situations (e.g. oil storage, complex railway networks). Automatically detecting potential risks by analyzing business errors in written documents is a relatively new approach. (Ament 2002) and (Weiss 1991) developed a number of useful methodological elements for authoring technical documents and error identification and correction. Similarly there are several tools for improving the quality and the coherence of requirements, in particular software and design requirements. Requirement traceability and update have also been the subject of many investigations. However, to the best of our knowledge, no tool with the functions offered by LELIE exists on the market.

LELIE is implemented in Dislog and runs on the <TextCoop> platform. A kernel is available for free for analysis and tests under a Creative Commons BY license.

The LELIE Approach and the Functions Offered

The main functional features of LELIE are:

-Authoring recommendations are taken into account in a modular way: any recommendation or subset of recommendations can be considered independently. They are also made flexible so that the necessity to follow them can depend on context. For example, if negation is not possible in instructions, there are however cases where it cannot be avoided because the positive counterpart of that negation cannot easily be formulated, e.g. *do not throw the acid into the sewer*: but *throw where?* Similarly, pronominal or temporal references are allowed if the referent is close and non-ambiguous.

-LELIE runs on <TextCoop> and realizes an analysis of the main discourse structures of procedural texts (presented in Chapter 2), therefore authoring recommendations may be parameterized and in particular may depend on discourse structures. For example deverbals may be allowed in titles, but not in instructions; the use of modals is the norm in requirements and warnings but must be avoided in instructions.

-Following observations in ergonomics, a specific effort has been realized concerning the well-formedness and the cohesion of discourse structures over entire documents (e.g. instructions or enumerations all written in the same way).

-The adequacy of the error analysis and diagnosis w.r.t. to the technical writer's working habits was also investigated so that the functions offered do correspond to his needs and to the way he works. The system is made flexible via an administrator interface so that the specificities of the domain (e.g. technical terms preferred to others) can be directly managed and updated by technical writers or validators and then inserted into the application lexicon.

-The production of procedures includes some controls on contents, in particular the contents of action verb arguments, as indicated in the second objective above, via the Arias prototypical action base. The objective is to avoid misconceptions, typos or confusions for syntactically and semantically well identified entities such as instruments, products, equipment, values, etc. This obviously requires domain knowledge, knowledge acquisition procedures from texts and coherence controls.

-There is no requirement analysis system based on language that can check authoring recommendations. The main products dedicated to requirement analysis are Doors and Doors-Trec, Objecteering, Reqtify and Craddle which are essentially text databases with query facilities and some traceability functions carried out via attributes (Chapter 6). However, there are ongoing attempts to improve Doors possibilities with the introduction of boilerplates or with some forms of conceptual analysis based on predefined attributes. These approaches or systems are relatively limited and leave little freedom to the author (e.g. the RQA system).

-The authoring tool we have developed includes facilities for French speaking authors who need to write in English, detecting the typical errors they make via forms of "language transfer" (Garnier 2010, 2011). This feature can be transposed to any language pair a priori, even if English remains the main language of technical documents.

The Lelie system is organized according to the following principles:

-The system is parameterized: the technical writer may choose the error types he wants to be checked, when and where, and the severity level and form of display for each error type. When there are several levels for a given error (for example there are several levels of severity associated with fuzzy terms), a local analysis of the error allows the production of an adapted error diagnosis,

-The system simply tags elements identified as errors, the correction is left to the author. However, some help or guidelines are offered. For example, guidelines to reformulate a negative sentence into a positive one are proposed,

-The way errors are displayed can be customized to the writer's habits, for example as comments in a Word document.

We present below a kernel system that deals with the most frequent and most common errors made by technical writers. This kernel needs an in-depth customization to the domain at stake. For example, the verbs used or the terminological preferences must be implemented for each industrial context. Finally, to avoid the variability of input document formats, the LELIE system input is a text structure with the minimal number of XML tags required by the error detection rules. Managing and transforming the original text formats (e.g. Microsoft Word) into this text format is not dealt with by the system, it is an interface problem, which may in fact be quite complex.

Risk Analysis and Prevention: the Context

Companies involved in sectors with a certain level of risk (nuclear, transport, food processing, chemistry) but also companies dealing with complex equipment or processes (food industry, health care, energy, etc.) or companies that have a strong quality insurance level, use and maintain a large number of technical documents. These documents are mainly procedure security requirements of various kinds, often represented as semi-structured documents. These documents have a large diversity in terms of formats, uses, functions, and management in the company. They often require complex authoring and control processes, a large number of actors, and complex quality operations to manage and guarantee their completeness, update, and customization.

Some of these documents may be issued in conjunction with control authorities (e.g. for health care, and product security), or they may require accreditations, certifications, following norms for example of type ISO 90001, 140001. These documents may also be organization notes, security plans, and more generally sets of procedures formalizing industrial processes (construction, quality controls, maintenance, logistics, staff hiring and training, etc.). In general, this set of documents is very large. It aims at making sure that a set of requirements and constraints (safety, quality, organizational, technical, etc.) are seriously taken into account to limit risks, be they injuries, ecological, social or financial. Their understandability and accuracy is therefore essential.

The consequences for labor of errors in technical documents are direct, often highly stressful and sometimes brutal: technical documentation must be continually renewed and updated, sometimes in very short time spans, as little as a few days for e.g. computer network security engineers. But even for those with less learning, e.g. the farmer in an emerging market hired to maintain or operate modern machinery, the corresponding know-how must be acquired quickly. The economic cost of a failed computer network is serious but much more horrific is the cost of untrained persons working with dangerous equipment. Recent studies in the area of maintenance (personal communication from Siveco) show that due to a lack of risk analysis, 80000 persons every year in India lose their lives, or undergo a major accident.

The impact of a lack of risk management on the environment is considerable as gas leaks, pipe leaks, e.g. as Union Carbide's accident in Bhopal and Chernobyl show. Less spectacular are other factors such as impoverished environments, due to:

-poorly maintained equipment that needs greater energy,

-poor equipment also means more equipment is needed to do the same job, fulfill the same production quotas, go around failures,

-equipment that is not properly installed and maintained can emit dangerous substances and gases.

Finally, Overall Equipment Effectiveness which refers to the losses and failures of various sources that occur in plants through breakdowns, losses in throughput and in yields is between 15 and 60% depending on the sector and the country. Most of the solutions reside in developing requirements and related controls in industrial procedures to detect problems related to risks.

All risks do not come from procedures and procedure careful analysis cannot prevent all risks. However, a recent analysis shows that about 78% of the risks come from ill-formed procedures (on the form or contents level). An analysis conducted in 2011 within the French RAMP project (involving EADS, Renault and EDF) shows that 56% of the risks come from a lack of clearly written and enforced risk prevention requirements, resulting in repair costs which can be as high as 82% of the initial development costs. The principle of checking for the quality of procedures via their analysis and their confrontation to safety requirements turns out to be an efficient and reliable strategy.

According to Siveco, among 377 technicians working in different areas of maintenance, 68% have detected major errors in technical documents leading to risks, 74% estimate that a good documentation is necessary while 64% admit that they realize procedures as best as they can, 54%

think that technical writers do not understand how technicians work, 78% admit that they need help quite frequently to overcome risky situations or gaps.

Requirements for large systems or organizations often look like a patchwork of recommendations produced by different authors. Requirements cover a large number of aspects: security, quality, productivity, reliability, etc. that have been defined at different periods by different groups of people, with substantially different competences, objectives, vocabularies, language habits and various visions of what an ideal procedure and risk management should be. This results in quite a high level of implicitness, incoherence, repetitions, fuzzy elements, and ambiguities. In the end, the taking into account of these gaps and misconceptions is on the operator's shoulders that has to manage priorities and missing data via his knowledge of the domain.

Finally, procedures are rarely produced from scratch but they are often produced from previously existing ones, with large risks of erroneous copy-paste. In a procedure life-cycle, there are often missing updates (in particular for those involving the cooperation of several equipment or processes), missing diagrams, confusions, and lack of user validation. Although correctly revising a procedure is costly, the gain estimate, with respect to possible failures, is estimated to 38% in the maintenance domain, according to Siveco. This is obviously is a major gain.

The market around risk prevention and management is very large, witness the number of associations and foundations that exist, the number of journals, conferences, shows, emerging projects around risk analysis. Risk analysis and prevention from written texts remains an open issue: there is a need to further analyze the problem, collect requirement corpora, and make recommendations about their form (style and contents) and organization. Everyday practice of technical writers, life cycle analysis, the development of models for validation processes and for the control of business rules must be investigated so that innovative solutions can be implemented.

Error Detection and Analysis in Procedural Texts

Let us now briefly present the types of errors LELIE can deal with, how these are implemented and what the performances are. The kernel of the system is presented in this chapter. This kernel needs several adaptations depending on the industrial context it is used in to be really useful.

Some rough indications on the global usefulness of the system are given. These are based on the types and the frequency of the main errors LELIE deals with. This section is an introduction to the first objective of LELIE. The implementation is available from the author under a "Creative Commons BY" license.

A Typology of Errors

In spite of several levels of human proofreading and validation, it turns out that texts still contain a large number of situations where recommendations are not followed. Reasons are analyzed in e.g. (Béguin, 2003), (Mollo et al. 2004, 2008). Via an analysis of the activity of technical writers, we have identified several layers of recurrent error types, which are not in general treated by standard text editors such as Word or Visio, the favorite text editors for procedures. Elements identified as errors in technical texts may perfectly be acceptable in ordinary language, such as fuzzy terms or negation.

Here is a list of categories of major errors which have been identified. The error types we present below are close to the principles given in Chapter 3, with some additional considerations and weights. Some errors are relevant for a whole document, whereas others are valid only in precise constructions:

-***General layout and organization of the document***, among which, most notably: the size of sentences and paragraphs; the homogeneity of the various forms of enumerations, the homogeneity of typography; the structure of titles; the presence of expected structures such as table of contents, and the text global organization following style recommendations such as correct position in the document of specific fields: safety precautions, prerequisites, etc.

-***Morphology and morphosyntax***: in general passive constructions and future must be avoided in instructions, modals are only possible in requirements, warnings and advice.

-***Lexical aspects***: include controls on the uses of fuzzy terms, inappropriate terms such as deverbals, light verb constructions, and detection of terms which cannot be conjoined e.g. in coordination. This latter point requires a semantic typing of lexical data or a domain ontology.

-***Grammatical restrictions and grammatical complexity***: the system detects various forms of negation uses, referential forms, sequences of conditional expressions, long sequences of coordination, complex noun complements, and complex embedding of relative clauses. All these constructions often make documents difficult to understand.

-***Uniformity and cohesion of style*** in general (i.e. independently of company guidelines) over a set of instructions, over titles and various lists of products and equipment, uniformity of expression of safety warnings and advice.

-***Discourse organization***: this level cannot be defined a priori for any industrial environment. It requires that the discourse structures in a paragraph or in an instruction are appropriately organized w.r.t. sentence and paragraph organization recommendations of the company at stake.

-***Document cohesion***: the uniformity of certain linguistic aspects must be checked, for example the list of verbs and connectors which are used or the verb position in an instruction w.r.t. its arguments. Document cohesion is a very large area of research and analysis that may involve complex controls,

-***Adequate use of business terms***: it is often required to use precise terms instead of general purpose ones. Similarly, some general language forms must be avoided while specifically designed others must be used. These are parameters of each company, possibly defined by type of task which must be specified for each use of the LELIE system.

Controls on semantic contents are more difficult to realize: they require a large diversity of domain knowledge and very accurate lexical data. The major semantic controls carried out in LELIE are those realized in the Objective 2 level of the system, where some argument contents are checked w.r.t. known practices and technical documentations.

In the LELIE approach, when a text is analyzed, the system annotates the original document: revisions are only made by technical writers, not by the system that does not have the expertise of the domain. Annotations can be e.g. in XML, as Word comments, or via colors in the text. When documents are inspected in batch mode, a score of the document global quality level can be produced. Tags are customized to authors, they are made explicit and easy to understand. These tags can convey a diagnosis formulated in linguistic terms or e.g. be expressed as very basic questions. For example, a sequence such as the following can be produced:

Move the vacuum compressor pump <to the area: WHICH ONE?>. For instance, close to the water storage or to the pool. <It: WHO? > should be on a higher level than <the source of water: VAGUE> and

<probably: VAGUE> 3 feet away. If you are working on a pool <it: WHO?> connects to the skimmer line.

Besides tags which must be as explicit as possible, colors can be used to indicate the severity level for the error considered (the same error, e.g. use of fuzzy term, can have several severity levels). The most severe errors must be corrected first. At the moment, the system proposes four levels of severity:

-ERROR: must be corrected,
-AVOID: preferably avoid this usage, think about an alternative,
-CHECK: this is not really bad, but it is recommended to make sure the statement is clear. This level is e.g. used to ask users to make sure that verb argument values are correct, when non-standard ones are found,
-ADVICE: possibly not the best language realization, but this is probably a minor problem. It is not clear that there are alternatives. However, if there are any, reformulations are welcome.

A few Case Studies

Let us now briefly investigate a few typical cases that make more explicit our methodology and the way errors are detected in the system. Only the main features of each error type are presented here, the comprehensive code being available.

The case of ***fuzzy terms*** is particularly significant of the way lexical errors can be detected and handled. The first thing to note is that there are several categories of fuzzy terms, in particular adverbs (manner, temporal, location, and modal adverbs), adjectives (*adapted, appropriate*) and determiners (*some, a few*), prepositions (*near*), a few verbs (*control, increase*) and nouns. These categories are not homogeneous in terms of fuzziness: determiners and prepositions are fuzzier than adjectives in general. The degree of fuzziness is also quite different from one term to another in a category. The context in which a fuzzy term is uttered may also have an influence on its severity level. For example *progressively* used in a short action (*progressively close the water pipe*) or used in an action that has a substantial length (*progressively heat the probe till 300 degrees Celsius are reached*) may entail different severity levels because the application of *progressively* may be more difficult to characterize for the second case. In the kernel of LELIE, the severity level is given a priori, but it can be adjusted when this kernel is adapted to an industrial context, where it is often largely enhanced. The context of fuzzy terms can be specified or acquired and associated with a specific severity level.

In Dislog, lexical entries are written as in DCGs:

```
lexfuzzy(Word,Features) -> Word.
```

Where Features encodes various types of information such as the category, the semantic class and the severity level:

```
lexfuzzy([from,time,to,time],[adv,temporal, error]) ->
                                        [from,time,to,time].
```

This lexical entry says that *from time to time* is a temporal adverb that generates an error of level ERROR when found in a text, in any context since no context is specified.

The rules, implemented in Dislog on the <TextCoop> platform, express in a declarative way how to identify fuzzy terms and what kind of message must be produced. Rules are in general very simple for lexical errors, here is a typical example:

```
rule(fuzzy-eng,          % name
E, S,                    % input-output
[ lexfuzzy(Fuzzy,[Type, Domain, error],E,S)],        % pattern
[],                                                  % no reasoning
[ '<b>', Fuzzy ,'</b>' , '<error attr="fuzzy term" >' ]).       % result
```

The system simply searches for a fuzzy term in the sentence being processed.

The case of ***pronominal references*** is quite different. It is clear that in any text, including technical ones, pronouns must be allowed. There are however situations where the referent of the pronoun is less easy to identify. It is not possible in our framework to evaluate the difficulty to find a pronoun antecedent for each situation. Therefore, the system detects a few prototypical situations which are often problematic. It produces for these cases an AVOID severity level, inviting the technical writer to make sure the pronoun is easy to interpret. The following situations have been identified as being *a priori* problematic (but these can be parameterized):

- -pronouns starting a sentence, an element of an enumeration or a cell in a chart,
- -the same pronoun occurring several times in a sentence, with the idea that it may refer to different objects,
- -the occurrence of several different pronouns in a sentence,
- -the occurrence of a pronoun without any acceptable antecedent (from a morphological and syntactic point of view) in a window of e.g. 10 words before it.
- -text zones which have a very high density of pronouns, independently of their type. Density can be parameterized, e.g. more than one pronoun every 8 words is a very high pronoun density that must be avoided.

Next, the analysis of the ***regularity of enumerative structures*** is also an important aspect of our system. By regularity, we mean the fact that each element in an enumeration has "about" the same structure. The goal is to facilitate the understanding of enumerations by readers by limiting their language processing efforts. In our approach, we consider the first elements in each enumeration element (in general 3 to 5 words, this is a parameter which can be adjusted), and control their syntactic regularity over an all the items of an enumeration structure. It is important to allow a certain flexibility in these first words. For example, if in a given enumeration, most items start by a verb in the infinitive form, it is important to allow e.g. a negative expression to start an enumeration (e.g.: *open / clean / do not throw / close*). We call this phenomenon ***modulation***: it is a lexical and syntactic function that allows some flexibility in enumerations. This principle is valid for any structure that requires some form of homogeneity. Modulation may also include discourse connectors or even discourse structures, for example a goal expression or a temporal connector may be possible before the verb without affecting the quality and the fluidity of the statements, as in:

1. *To get a brighter color, add salt*
2. *then boil for 2 minutes.*

The last case we briefly consider in this section is the ***detection of discourse structure patterns that do not follow guidelines***. This case is in general complex to resolve, but it turns out to be somewhat feasible in our case because a number of discourse structures can be identified by LELIE, following e.g. the rules given in Chapter 2. A regular organization of discourse structures with respect to a task to realize limits the document cognitive complexity and allows users to concentrate on the task rather than spending efforts understanding the text. Another important feature is the use and the position of warnings in a text and their justification(s). For example, the LELIE system can make sure that any warning is immediately followed by its support, the justification of the warning. Another situation is the organization of the environment of an action. For example, guidelines may require the following sequence, when appropriate:

-context or conditions of an action,
-actions to carry out (ordered set of instructions),
-justifications and precautions to take (warnings).

If, in a text, a different structure is found, e.g. the instructions come after the justifications, then an error message can be produced. Such guidelines are implemented by means of discourse schemas encoded in

Dislog rules. For example, the above example is implemented by the following sequence of XML tags:

```
[......
< condition > ..... < /condition >
        < instruction > ..... </instruction >
                < justification > ..... < /justification >
                ............ ]
```

Any sequence of such tags found with a different order is indicated to the technical writer with a priori an AVOID severity level.

Some Elements of an Evaluation

It is difficult to *a priori* measure the efficiency of our model and of our implementation since it needs to be customized to an industrial environment to be really effective. This is an ongoing process which is being carried out with a few companies. This process requires a lot of time. However, we can give the following general evaluation we carried out on a relatively small generic test corpus in French:

Error type	Number manually annotated	Recall %	Precision %
Fuzzy terms	58	89	97
Deverbals	23	94	95
Modals	6	98	100
Pronouns with unclear antecedents	20	91	93
negation	44	100	100
Heavy noun complements	39	86	94
Sentences too long (> 40 words)	99	91	96

Table 7-1 Error detection accuracy in Lelie

Results are satisfactory in general w.r.t. the manually annotated errors. Recall may be somewhat low in some cases, but our strategy was to favor precision over recall. To improve the overall quality of some errors, it may be necessary to develop some local syntactic analysis. It is also crucial to develop some flexibility in the analysis of errors. For example, pronouns in impersonal configurations (e.g. *it*) must not be tagged as errors. In some cases, deverbals (nouns derived from verbs) could be used instead of the corresponding verb because they are very common (e.g. *reception* instead of *receive*). For complex noun complements, confusions may occur with complex technical terms which should not be counted as noun complements. Finally, sentence length must be a more complex measure than just the number of words it has. The measure of the length needs to include the complexity of the words (technical versus common language) and of the syntactic constructions.

Most technical writers recognize the usefulness of such a system. However, the system needs a very detailed tuning to really recognize structures which are errors. At the moment we still have a lot of noise: some structures annotated as erroneous are not incorrect or their severity level is low and no correction is needed. This is for example the case of the use of negation, which cannot be avoided in certain, unpredictable situations, or of fuzzy terms which, depending on context, show very different levels of fuzziness. Tuning the errors and adapting the system is part of its industrial customization, this task requires a lot of efforts and time.

Nevertheless, even after some tuning, our system still detects quite a large number of error situations which must be corrected. We give below some figures related the detection of several errors in an implementation we have developed for three companies. For each error type, we give its average frequency for 1000 lines of text (corresponding to about 30 000 words) computed from different texts in each company. Results are for French. This analysis shows major differences between companies. To keep these companies anonymous, we use here the letters A, B and C to identify them. The results can be summarized as follows:

Error type	Average frequency For 1000 lines	A	B	C
Fuzzy terms	66	44	89	49
deverbals	29	24	14	42
modals	5	0	12	0
Light verb constructions	2	2	2	3
Verb diversity	average	low	high	low
Pronoun reference	22	4	48	2
Negation in instructions	52	8	109	9
Complex subordinate clauses	7	0	5	0
Incorrect position of some Terms (e.g. misplaced verbs)	56	57	82	33

Too many coordination in a sentence	6	0	10	0
Heavy noun complements	36	28	62	15
Passive constructions to avoid	34	16	72	4
Future tense to avoid	2	2	4	1
Sentences too long (beyond 40 words)	108	16	221	24
Irregular forms of enumerations	average	low	high	Aver age
Incorrect references to other sections	13	33	22	2

Table 7-2 Error Frequency in various corpora

As the reader may note it, the distribution of errors is quite different from a company to another. Company A has relatively simple documents, with short sentences, while company B has very complex texts, which may have suffered from a large number of revision and validation steps. Company C has quite complex texts, but these have been revised by experts in document authoring. Nevertheless, a number of errors remain to be corrected.

User Reactions

It is now of much interest to analyze how technical writers react to the errors which are displayed in their texts. An objective measure (besides their satisfaction or dissatisfaction) is to count the number of errors which have been corrected, how, and how much time it took to correct each error. A closer look at the way technical writers behave when they get error messages reveals several strategies, which are roughly the following:

-an error has been found relevant and has indeed been appropriately corrected. Furthermore, the writer may wish to keep track of his correction for similar situations he may find in the future for him or to share with the technical writers around him,

-an error has been found relevant, but considering the text segment at stake, the writer realizes that the correction must be done on a larger scale because a whole portion of text around the error deserves improvement,

-an error has been found relevant and has been corrected, but it has generated another error. This point raises another issue: the order in which corrections should be made, since some corrections may entail new errors,

-an error has been found relevant but the author has no correction in mind, or he does not fully understand the error or does not see why it is an error. The error is not corrected in the text. The writer may also look for similar errors in the text to see if and how they have been corrected,

-an error that the writer does not want to correct, for various reasons, in particular because it is minor or because it does not alter the understanding of the sentence,

-an error indicated by the system, but that turns out to be a wrong diagnosis: the text span is perfectly correct.

The development of these scenarios is important when constructing a real, operational system for technical writers. Memorizing the corrections already carried out and their context is an important issue, so that the correction phase can be improved.

Conclusion

The LELIE system presented here is still in an early stage of development: although a relatively satisfactory kernel has been developed and tested, it needs to get a lot of maturity via its customization to various industrial environments. If the analysis of the form, from lexical issues to style, is relatively well mastered, the analysis of the contents remains a major challenge which still requires research in language processing and artificial intelligence.

Customization experiments are ongoing in various areas, most notably in the energy, transportation and food processing domains. Documents considered are either procedures or sets of requirements. An investigation of the integration of this tool in companies' authoring systems when they already exist, or in their information system, is a major task that must be carried out with great care, involving studies in ergonomics, since this tool changes the way technical writers work.

The kernel of Lelie is freely available for test and commerce under a Creative Commons BY license.

BIBLIOGRAPHY

Adam, J.M. 1987, "Types de Sequences Textuelles Elementaires", Pratiques n°56, Metz.

Alred, G. J., Brusaw, C. T., and Walter E. O. 2012, *Handbook of Technical Writing*. St Martin's Press, New York.

Ashley, K.,D., Desai, R., Levine, J.M. 2002, *Teaching case-based argumentation concepts using dialectic arguments vs. didactic explanations*, ITS 2002, Lecture notes in computer science.

Ament, K. 2002, *Single Sourcing. Building modular documentation*, W. Andrew Pub.

Amgoud, L., Parsons and S., Maudet, N. 2001, Arguments, Dialogue, and Negotiation, in: 14th European Conference on Artificial Intelligence, Berlin.

Amgoud, L., Bonnefon, J.F., Prade, H. 2005, An Argumentation-based Approach to Multiple Criteria Decision, in 8th European Conference on Symbolic and Quantitative Approaches to Reasoning with Uncertainty, ECSQARU'2005, Barcelona.

Aouladomar, F. 2005, Towards Answering Procedural Questions, in : KRAQ'05 - IJCAI workshop, Edinburgh, F. Benamara, P. Saint-Dizier (Eds.), pp. 24-36.

—. 2005, A Semantic Analysis of Instructional Texts, IWCS05, Tilburg.

Bal, B.K. and Saint-Dizier, P. 2010, Towards Building Annotated Resources for Analyzing Opinions and Argumentation in News Editorial, LREC, Malta.

Barcellini, F., Gross, C., Albert, C. and Saint-Dizier, P. 2012, Risk Analysis and Prevention: LELIE, a Tool dedicated to Procedure and Requirement Authoring, LREC, Istanbul.

Barenfanger, M. and Hilbert, M. 2006, Cues and constraints for the relational discourse analysis of complex text types – the role of logical and generic document structure, proceedings CID'06.

Béguin, P. Design as a mutual learning process between users and designers Interacting with computers, 15 (6), 2003.

Benamara, F. and Saint-Dizier, P., Advanced Relaxation for Cooperative Question Answering. in New Directions in Question Answering, Mark Maybury (ed), MIT Press, 234-254, 2004.

Bieger, G.R. and Glock, M.D. 1984-1985, "The Information Content of Picture-text Instructions", Journal of Experimental Education, 53, 68-75.

Bourse, S. and Saint-Dizier, P. 2011, "The language of explanation dedicated to technical documents", Syntagma, vol. 27, 2011..

Buddenberg, Arnold. 2011, Guidelines for writing requirements. (personal communication).

Canitrot, M., Roger, PY and Saint-Dizier, P. 2011, How-To Question-Answering: hints on extraction, LTC conference, Poznan.

Caminada, M. and Amgoud, L. 2007, "On the evaluation of argumentation formalisms", Artificial Intelligence Journal, V.171 (5-6), 286-310.

Carlson, L., Marcu, D., Okurowski, M.E. 2001, Building a Discourse-Tagged Corpus in the Framework of Rhetorical Structure Theory. In Proceedings of the 2nd SIGdial Workshop on Discourse and Dialog, Aalborg.

Chomsky, N. 1986, *Barriers*, Linguistic Inquiry Monograph nb. 13, MIT Press.

—. 1990, *Some concepts and consequences of the theory of Government and Binding*, Linguistic Inquiry Monograph nb. 6, MIT Press.

Colmerauer, A. 1978, Metamorphosis Grammars, in Natural language understanding by computers, L. Bolc (ed.), LNCS no. 63, Springer Verlag.

Couper-Kuhlen, E. and Kortmann, B. 2000, *Cause, Condition, Concession, Contrast: Cognitive and Discourse Perspectives,* (Topics in English Linguistics, No 33), de Gryuter.

Cruse, A. 1986, *Lexical Semantics*, Cambridge University press.

Davidson, D. 1980, *Essays on Actions and Events*, Oxford: Oxford University Press.

Declerck, R., and Reed, S. 2001, *Conditionals: A comprehensive empirical analysis*, W. de Gruyter.

Delin, J., Hartley, A., Paris, C., Scott, D. and Vander Linden, K. 1994, Expressing Procedural Relationships in Multilingual Instructions, Proceedings of the Seventh International Workshop on Natural Language Generation, pp. 61-70, USA.

Delpech, E. and Saint-Dizier, P. 2008, Investigating the structure of procedural texts for answering How-to Questions, Language Resources and Evaluation Conference (LREC), Marrakech, European Language Resources Association (ELRA).

Di Eugenio, B. and Webber, B.L. 1996, "Pragmatic Overloading in Natural Language Instructions", International Journal of Expert Systems.

Dixon, R.M.W. 2000, A typology of causatives: form, syntax and meaning, in Changing Valency: Case Studies in Transitivity, Dixon, R.M.W. and Alexandra Y. Aikhenvald, eds.: 30–83. New York: Cambridge University Press.

Donin, J., Bracewell, R. J., Frederiksen, C. H. and Dillinger, M. 1992, "Students' Strategies for Writing Instructions: Organizing Conceptual Information in text", Written Communication 9, 209-236.

Dowty, D. 1991, "Thematic Proto-roles and Argument Selection", Language, vol. 67(3).

Eemeren, F.H. and van Grootendorst, R. 1984, *Speech acts in argumentative discussions: A theoretical model for the analysis of discussions directed towards solving conflicts of opinion*, Foris Publications.

Eemeren, F.H. and van Grootendorst, R. 1992, *Argumentation, communication, and fallacies: A pragma-dialectical perspective*, Lawrence Erlbaum Associates.

Eemeren, F.H. van, (ed). 2002,, *Advances in pragma-dialectics*, Newport News, Vale Press.

Fellbaum, C. 1998, *WordNet An Electronic Lexical Database*, The MIT Press.

Fontan, L. and Saint-Dizier, P. 2008, Analyzing the explanation structure of procedural texts: dealing with Advices and Warnings, International Symposium on Text Semantics (STEP 2008), Johan Bos (Eds.), Association for Computational Linguistics (ACL).

Ferrari, G. 1988, Preliminary steps toward the creation of a discourse and text resource, In Proceedings of the First International Conference on Language Resources and Evaluation (LREC), Granada.

Fiedler, A. and Horacek, H. 2001, Argumentation in Explanations to Logical Problems, in Proceedings of ICCS 2001, Springer LNCS 2073, pp. 969–978.

Garcia-Villalba, M. and Saint-Dizier, P. 2012, Some Facets of Argument Mining for Opinion Analysis, in proceedings of COMMA'12, IOS Press, Vienna.

Gardent, C. 1997, Discourse tree adjoining grammars, report nb. 89, Univ. Saarlandes, Saarbrucken.

Garnier, M. 2010, Correcting errors produced by French speakers: the case of misplaced adverbs, Calico, Amherst.

—. 2011, Correcting errors in N+N structures in the production of French users of English, EuroCall, Nottingham.

Gazdar, G. and Mellish, C. 1989, Natural Language Processing in Prolog: An Introduction to Computational Linguistics, Addison Wesley.

Gnesi, S. and Lami, G., 2005, "An Automatic Tool for the Analysis of Natural Language Requirements", in IJCSSE (International Journal of Computer Systems Science & Engineering) special issue, Volume 20(1).

Grady, J. O. 2006, *System Requirements Analysis*, Academic Press, USA.

Grice, H. P. 1978, Logic and Conversation, in P. Cole and J. L. Morgan (eds) Syntax and Semantics vol. 3, Speech Acts, Academic Press 113-127.

Grosz, B. and Sidner, C. 1986, "Attention, intention and the structure of discourse", Computational Linguistics 12(3).

Hull,E., Jackson,K. and Dick, J. 2011, *Requirements Engineering*, Springer.

Jin, W., Simmons, R. 1987, Question Answering with Rhetorical Relations, IEEE conf. on AI.

Helbig., H. 2005, *Knowledge representation and the semantics of natural language.* Cognitive Technologies, Springer-Verlag.

Keil, F.C. and Wilson, R.A. 2000, *Explanation and Cognition*, Bradford Book.

Kintsch, W. 1988, "The Role of Knowledge in Discourse Comprehension: A Construction Integration Model", Psychological Review, vol. 95(2).

Kosseim, L. and Lapalme, G. 2000, "Choosing Rhetorical Structures to Plan Instructional Texts", Computational Intelligence, Blackwell, Boston.

Lakoff, R. 1971, If, ands and buts about conjunction, Studies in Linguistic Semantics, Holt, Reinhart and Winston (ed) MIT Press.

Lasnik, H. and Uriagereka, J. 1988, *A Course in GB syntax*, MIT Press, 1988.

Lemarie, J., Lorch, R. F., Eyrolle, H. and Virbel, J. 2008, "SARA: A text-based and reader-based theory of text signalling", Educational Psychologist, 43, 27.

Luc, C., Mojahid, M., Virbel, J., Garcia-Debanc, C. and Pery-Woodley, M-P. 1999, *A Linguistic Approach to Some Parameters of Layout: A study of enumerations*, In R. Powerand D. Scott (Eds.), Using Layout for the Generation, Understanding or Retrieval of Documents, AAAI 1999 Fall Symposium, pp. 20-29.

Longacre, R. 1982, "Discourse Typology in Relation to Language Typology", Sture, Allen (ed.), Text Processing, Proceeding of Nobel Symposium 51, Stockholm, Almquist and Wiksell, 457-486.

Mann, W. and Thompson, S. 1988, "Rhetorical Structure Theory: Towards a Functional Theory of Text Organisation", TEXT 8 (3) pp. 243-281.

Mann, W. and Thompson, S.A. (eds) 1992, *Discourse Description: diverse linguistic analyses of a fund raising text*, John Benjamins.
Marcu, D, 1997, The Rhetorical Parsing of Natural Language Texts, proceedings of ACL97.
—. 2000, *The Theory and Practice of Discourse Parsing and Summarization*, MIT Press.
—. 2002, Au unsupervised approach to recognizing Discourse relations, proceedings ACL02.
Masthoff, J., Reed, C. and Grasso, F. (eds) 2008, *Symposium on Persuasive Technology,* in conjunction with the AISB 2008, Convention Communication, Interaction and Social Intelligence, Aberdeen.
Miltasaki, E., Prasad, R., Joshi, A. and Webber, B. 2004, Annotating Discourse Connectives and Their Arguments, new frontiers in NLP.
Moeschler, J. 2007, The role of explicature in communication and in intercultural communication, in Kecskes I. et al. (eds), Explorations in Pragmatics, Linguistic, Cognitive and Intercultural Aspects, Berlin, Mouton de Gruyter.
—. 2002, Speech act theory and the analysis of conversation, in Vandervecken D. et al. (eds), Essays in Speech Act Theory, Amsterdam, John Benjamins.
Mollo, V. and Falzon, P. 2004, "Auto and allo-confrontation as tools for reflective activities", Applied Ergonomics, 35 (6), 531-540.
Nuseibeh, B. and Easterbrook, S. 2000, "Requirements Engineering: A Roadmap", ICSE'00 Proceedings of the 22nd international conference on Software engineering, P.37-46.
O'Brien, Sharon, 2003, Controlling Controlled English, An Analysis of Several Controlled Language Rule Sets. School of Applied Language and Intercultural Studies Dublin City University Dublin 9, Ireland.
Pereira, F. 1981, "Extraposition Grammars", Computational Linguistics, vol. 9-4.
Pereira, F. and Warren, D. 1980, "Definite Clause Grammars for Language Analysis", Artificial Intelligence vol. 13(3).
Pohl K. 2010, *Requirements Engineering: Fundamentals, Principles, and Techniques*, Springer Publishing Company.
Pollock, J.L. 1974, Knowledge and Justification, Princeton university Press.
Redeker, G. 1990, Ideational and Pragmatic Markers of Discourse Structure, Journal of Pragmatics, vol. 14.
Reed, C. 1988, Generating Arguments in Natural Language, PhD dissertation, University College, London.

Reed, C.A. and Long, D.P. 1997, Content Ordering in the Generation of Persuasive Discourse, in Proceedings of 15th International Joint Conference on Artificial Intelligence, Nagoya, Japan.

Reed, C.A. and Long, D.P. 1998, Generating the Structure of Argument, in Proceedings of the 17th International Conference on Computational Linguistics and 36th Annual Meeting of the Association for Computational Linguistics (COLING-ACL98), Montreal, Canada.

Reed, C. and Grasso, F. 2007, "Recent Advances in Computational Models of Natural Argument", International Journal of Intelligent Systems, 22(1).

Rosner, D. and Stede, M. 1992, Customizing RST for the Automatic Production of Technical Manuals, in R. Dale, E. Hovy, D. Rosner and O. Stock eds., Aspects of Automated Natural Language Generation, Lecture Notes in Artificial Intelligence, pp. 199-214, Springler-Verlag.

Saaba A. and Sawamura, H. 2008, Argument Mining Using Highly Structured Argument Repertoire, proceedings EDM08, Niigata.

Sage, A.P. and Rouse, W.B. 2009, *Handbook of Systems Engineering and Management*, 2nd Edition, Wiley, USA.

Saito, M., Yamamoto, K. and Sekine, S. 2006, Using Phrasal Patterns to Identify Discourse Relations, proceedings ACL06.

Saint-Dizier, P. 1994, *Advanced Logic programming for language processing*, Academic Press.

Sampaio, A., Loughran, N., Rashid, A. and Rayson, P. 2005, Mining Aspects in Requirements, Early Aspects 2005: Aspect-Oriented Requirements Engineering and Architecture Design Workshop, Chicago.

Schank, R. 1986, *Explanation Patterns: Understanding Mechanically and Creatively*, Laurence Erlbaum.

Schauer, H. 2006, From elementary discourse units to complex ones, Sigdial workshop, ACL06.

Schriver, K. A. 1989, Evaluating text quality: The continuum from text-focused to reader focused methods, IEEE Transactions on Professional Communication, 32, 238-255.

Searle, J. R. and Vanderveken, D. 1985, *Foundations of Illocutionary Logic,* Cambridge University Press.

Sierra, G., Alarcon, R., Aguilar, C. and Bach, C. 2008, "Definitional verbal patterns for semantic relation extraction", Journal of terminology, 14-1.

Spenader, J. and Lobanova, A. 2007, Reliable Discourse Markers for Contrast. Eighth International Workshop on Computational Semantics, Tilburg.

Stabler, E. 1992, *The logical approach to syntax*, MIT Press.

Stede, M. 2012, *Discourse Processing*, Morgan and Claypool Publishers.

Takechi, M., Tokunaga, T., Matsumoto, Y. and Tanaka, H. 2003, Feature Selection in Categorizing Procedural Expressions, The Sixth International Workshop on Information Retrieval with Asian Languages (IRAL2003), pp.49-56.

Talmy, L. 2001, *Towards a Cognitive Semantics*, vol. 1 and 2, MIT Press.

Taboada, M. and Mann, W.C. 2006, "Rhetorical Structure Theory: Looking back and moving ahead", Discourse Studies, 8(3), 423-459.

Taboada, M. 2006, "Discourse markers as signals (or not) of rhetorical relations", Journal of Pragmatics, 38:567–592, 2006.

Van der Linden, K. 1993, Speaking of Actions Choosing Rhetorical Status and Grammatical Form in Instructional Text Generation Thesis, University of Colorado.

Van Dijk, T.A. 1980, *Macrostructures*, Hillsdale, NJ: Lawrence Erlbaum Associates.

Walton, D. 1992, *The Place of Emotion in Argument*, Pennsylvania state university press.

Walton, D., Reed, C. and Macagno, F. 2008, *Argumentation Schemes*, Cambridge University Press.

Webber, B.L. and Di Eugenio, B. 1990, Free Adjuncts in Natural Language Instructions, Proceedings COLING-90, Helsinki.

Webber, B. 2004, "D-LTAG: extending lexicalized TAGs to Discourse", Cognitive Science 28, pp. 751-779, Elsevier.

Weiss, Edmond H. 1990, *Practical exercises for technical writing*, The Oryx Press, Westport.

—. 1991, *How to write usable user documentation*, The Oryx Press, Westport.

Wierzbicka, A. 1987, *English Speech Act Verbs*, Academic Press.

Wolf, F. and Gibson, E. 2005, "Representing Discourse Coherence: A Corpus-Based Study", Computational Linguistics 31(2): 249_288.

Wright, von G.H. 2004, *Explanation and understanding*, Cornell university Press.

Wright, S.E. and Budin G. 2001, *Handbook of Terminology Management: Application-oriented Terminology Management*, volume 2. Kent State University. University of Vienna. p.872.

Zuckerman, I., McConachy, R. and Korb, K. 2000, Using Argumentation Strategies in Automatic Argument Generation, INLG00.

IEEE Std 830-1993, *Recommended Practice for Software Requirements Specifications*, December 2, 1993.

References with Internet links

Wyner, Adam, Krasimir Angelov, Guntis Barzdins, Danica Damljanovic, Brian Davis, Norbert Fuchs, Stefan Hoefler, Ken Jones, Kaarel Kaljurand, Tobias Kuhn, Martin Luts, Jonathan Pool, Mike Rosner, Rolf Schwitter, and John Sowa. 2010. On Controlled Natural Languages: Properties and Prospects.

Controlled Languages. A research note by Namahn. 2002. Accessed on 04.07.2012.
http://www.namahn.com/resources/documents/note-CL.pdf

Quintal, Poppy. 2002. AECMA Simplified English. PLAIN Conference. Toronto. Accessed on 04.07.2012.
http://www.nald.ca/library/research/plain2/aecma/aecma.pdf

Unwalla, Mike. 2004. AECMA Simplified English. TechScribe. Accessed on 04.07.2012.
http://www.techscribe.co.uk/ta/aecma-simplified-english.pdf

What is Simplified Technical English? Accessed on 04.07.2012.
http://www.boeing.com/phantom/sechecker/se.html

Brown, Russ. Simplified English. 2000. Accessed on 04.07.2012.
http://www.userlab.com/Downloads/SE.pdf

Barthe, Kathy. 2004. ASD (AECMA) Simplified English. Extracts from the Airbus France Training Course for Authors. Accessed on 04.07.2012.
http://cpf.s1000d.org/events/user_forum/vaxjo/22am01A_SE%20TutorialWeb.pdf

Muegge, Uwe. http://www.muegge.cc/controlled-language.htm. Accessed on 04.07.2012.

Wojcik, Richard H., Hoard, James E. Controlled Languages in Industry. In Survey of the state of the art in human language technology. Chapter 7. Accessed on 04.07.2012.
http://www.lt-world.org/hlt-survey/ltw-chapter7-6.pdf .
http://www.cslu.ogi.edu/HLTsurvey/ch7node8.html

CONTRIBUTORS

The contributors to this book are members of the ANR funded LELIE project, presented in Chapter 7 of this book.

Camille ALBERT teaches English Literature and Linguistics in Toulouse. She has been involved in the elaboration of writing practices for technical documents and has published conference papers in this area.

Mathide JANIER is a PhD student currently at Dundee University, Scotland. She has experience is language resource development and in argumentation theory. She is the co-author of several papers in these areas.

Juyeon KANG has a PhD in linguistics (Paris 4), she is now a senior researcher in the Prometil Company in Toulouse, France. She is an expert of Categorial Grammars, language processing technology, and requirements. She is the author of several conference publications in these areas.

Patrick SAINT-DIZIER, PhD, is a senior researcher in Computational Linguistics at IRIT-CNRS in Toulouse, France, where he is the head of the ILPL research group (language processing and logic programming). He is the author or the editor of several books and journal articles in language processing and in logic programming.

INDEX